COME FLY WITH ME

EXPERIENCES OF AN AIRMAN IN WORLD WAR II

by
LLOYD KRUEGER, 1ST LIEUTENANT
U.S. ARMY AIRFORCE

toExcel
San Jose New York Lincoln Shanghai

Come Fly With Me

All Rights Reserved. Copyright © 1992, 2000 by Lloyd O. Krueger

No part of this book may be reproduced or transmitted in any form or by any means, graphic, electronic, or mechanical, including photocopying, recording, taping, or by any information storage or retrieval system, without the permission in writing from the publisher.

This edition published by toExcel Press,
an imprint of iUniverse.com, Inc.

For information address:
iUniverse.com, Inc.
620 North 48th Street
Suite 201
Lincoln, NE 68504-3467
www.iuniverse.com

ISBN: 0-595-09135-0

This book is dedicated to my Friend, my Pal, my Companion, my Wife...Norma Ann. With her dedication, patience, and understanding, all things are possible.

Give it a Chance

We answered the call,
Of a country in need.
We accepted the challenge,
To see nations freed.

We gave up our youth,
So others survive,
We believed in the cause,
For the dictators' demise.

We have only to learn,
The need to be responsible.
A world at peace,
Makes all things possible.

We have the knowledge,
But we need desire,
To lay down our arms,
For a life to aspire.

This world we live in,
Though large in scope,
Grows smaller each day,
Where all have to cope.

Let's take the time,
And make every effort.
To learn from the past,
We're really not different.

Each race and each culture,
Has much to contribute,
So let's give it a chance,
Pay peace its due tribute.

My comrades in arms,
Who gave up their lives.
Wanted a world,
For all, to survive.

lloyd o. krueger

TABLE OF CONTENTS

Title	Page
U.S. Air Force Cadet	1
Preflight School	11
Deutschland and Beyond	19
In Retrospect	33
B-17 Flying Fortress	43
Box B to Big B	53
"Know thy Enemy"	67
D-Day June 6, 1944	79
The No-Ball Target	89
Plane Number 297334	99
French Maquis	105
The Girl I Left Behind	111
Mission Number 30—"A Milk Run"	121
Blitz over Politz	129
Fear—Not Just Another Emotion	135
Nose Art and Nicknames	145
The Curtain Drops	157
Returning Home	163
Far Away Places	173
95th Bomb Group Reunion	185
Epilogue	189

THE PRELUDE

For one reason or another, this story concerns the experiences of one airman from the 8th Air Force and his part in World War II. The part any one person plays in a major war, such as the terrible one fought in Europe and the Pacific, has to be almost insignificant. However, for each particular participant, this catastrophe left an indelible mark on each of us. Those who were fortunate to have survived are obviously grateful, but the memories conjured by such a war are deep and lasting. Now, 47 years later, it is important to put each of these many recollections together in order to paint a complete picture of this period in my life.

My own part in this important period of history took place between July 1942 and October of 1945. The chapters that follow will give a typical account of how one individual was plucked out of society and turned into an efficient tool of war. The millions of Americans and other Allies, as well as those from the Axis Powers, have similar stories to tell. Unfortunately, most of these memories and experiences will never be related or passed on. If all of these anecdotes could be recounted and recorded, perhaps this world would realize that war is never a solution. The waste of human life, the suffering, and the utter destruction has only negative connotations.

When the United States entered the war and our country called on its youth to volunteer or be called up by the Selective Service System (draft), I recalled the advice my father gave me (he had volunteered to serve in the Infantry in the Seventh Division in France during World War I). His advice to my two brothers and me was "never volunteer" and most important, "stay out of the infantry." His memories of trench warfare gave him a strong prejudice that was reflected in his admonition to "stay out of the infantry." I had an early desire to become an aeronautical engineer so my choice to join the Air Force was logical. My brothers, for their own reasons, both volunteered for the U.S. Coast Guard.

My story will take me from my home in the north central part of Wisconsin; through my training in the Air Force Cadets; my trip to Europe; actual combat; my return to the States; my stint in the Air Transport Command; and finally, my discharge. The fact that I chose the Air Force and not some other branch of service had nothing to do with my determination or dedication. I would have put forth the same effort wherever my country desired my services. The Air Force, because of my early interests, held special appeals in each of its many branches. I had no idea where the military felt I truly belonged. Though I had aspirations of actually flying, I was prepared to be a part of a ground crew, just to be near planes. This now is my story......

Note: It is important to know and realize that each Chapter was originally meant as a single story, each as a separate entity, and not intended for publication. Many Air Force Veterans who read these stories encouraged the author to include them in the form of a book. It was decided to include each of these stories in the sequence in which they were written, with *no* attempt to develope a chronological order.

 U.S. Air Force Cadet

On July 23, 1942, I made a special trip to the Post Office in my home town, Wausau, Wisconsin, to visit the local recruiting office. I went there with the full intention of enlisting in the U.S. Army Air Force, but I had planned to act indifferent to any of the recruiting personnel to get their best pitch on why I should make that decision. I signed the necessary documents. Some months earlier, while I was attending the University of Wisconsin, I had registered for the draft and now, just a week after enlisting, I received notice that I was to report for induction into the Army. The date that they gave for this momentous occasion was August 2nd, 1942. This trip to the Post Office was none too soon.

The four members of the Air Force recruiting team greeted me in their snazzy uniforms and were most cordial. They were clean shaven, bubbling with enthusiasm, covered with battle ribbons, and made one hell of an impression. The picture they described of cadet life in the Air Force and ultimately sitting at the controls of a fighter plane sounded completely irresistible. It was not difficult to sign the necessary papers that would get me unconditionally and permanently involved. In the months that followed, I would get flash backs and moments of regret. Now that I had put my pen to paper I had only to wait until I was notified where and when my training would begin.

Over five months would pass as I impatiently waited for my orders. During this period I was hired and quit five different jobs. I did not want to work up to the last moment before leaving for the wars so I would take my leave from mundane jobs and live it up. When I ran low on money I'd get another job. Finally, early in January 1943, I was notified that on January 17 that I was to go to Chicago aboard the Milwaukee Road Hiawatha train. At a large federal building, I went to the designated office and immediately learned that I was not the only individual who had the bright idea to learn to fly at government expense. Greg Turner, another man from Wausau, and I opened the door and were astounded to see over two hundred fellows our age. This was my very first realization that we were to be handled and treated like a herd of cattle. We were yelled at, barked at, pushed in various directions, given orders and instructions faster than we could possibly comprehend, and yes, we were made to feel that "we had been had." What in hell had I volunteered for?

The one instruction that came through loud and clear was the fact that we would board a train at 7:15 PM at the Union Depot and head for Nashville, Tennessee. I can still remember the expressions on most of the guys' faces during the train ride......each was thinking the same as me, "there's no turning back now." The base at Nashville consisted of over one hundred, two-story barracks painted a dirty white, several large mess halls, several buildings used for special purposes, and one huge drill field. The weather on this day of arrival was appropriate for this auspicious occasion; it was gray and drizzling. Mud was everywhere, with small piles of snow covered with black soot. As soon as we were off the train, we were ordered to line up and "dress right." What in hell is "dress right." With a sergeant's nose pressed against yours and his warm smelly breath screaming further instructions, it wasn't too hard to learn. This intimidation technique was used often the first couple of days. The sun took several weeks to find this base in Nashville. It took the same amount of time before we were issued uniforms. We marched and drilled for nearly two weeks in our civilian clothes. What a motley looking military unit. The extremely high humidity made the damp cold air penetrate ever fiber of my being. I do believe that I have never been so cold and miserable, despite the fact that I came from northern Wisconsin. To make matters even worse, we saw most of the native residents of Nashville walking around in shirt sleeves. This was not the picture I visualized that morning in the recruiting office. My morale was sinking fast.

The third day on the Base we were herded down to what might be referred to as a barber shop. I was one of the few recruits who didn't get the shock of having their locks removed. I had a crew cut or "butch" style hair cut ever since junior high school days. In a matter of minutes each guy began to look scalped. The barbers were literally ankle deep in hair and the huge room was filled with groans and moans. When uniforms were finally issued, little or no attention was given to matching size to each individual. Winter items of clothing were thrown on outstretched arms and we were encouraged to keep moving. Shoes were the only thing they handed out that resembled the proper size. The sleeves on my overcoat were several inches below my finger tips and my pants had legs meant for a six foot six giant. Fortunately, I had been taught to sew and had the foresight to bring a kit along that had needles, thread, and a small pair of scissors. With this kit I became an instant tailor and was able to rediscover my hands and feet by shortening my new overcoat and pants. Others had to wait for a leave to find tailors in Nashville. I was truly happy that I entered the service with a sense of humor and was able to cultivate a disposition that permitted me to have a capricious frame of mind that had no trouble in making light of snafued situations. My only hope was that my German foes would be subjected to the same problems and treatment.

Our daily routine was to rise early each morning in the dark, hurry everywhere and be compelled to wait, march over every square foot of the drill field that was the size of ten football fields, eat food that was literally thrown at you, or just lay around in our barracks on uncomfortable cots and listen to gripes in the various dialects from individuals from each corner of our country. The only common denominator each of us had was the opinion of how this mans' army was run. There was no special feeling of being an aviation cadet. Our drill instructors constantly reminded us that the only thing lower than our rank as a cadet was a "yard bird," which was supposed to be several grades below a "buck private" in the regular army.

Finally, on February 17, 1943, exactly one month after we arrived in Nashville, Tennessee, we all boarded a troop train. This train was taking us to Pre-flight School at San Antonio, Texas. The definition of a troop train is a large collection of old passenger cars connected to a worn out steam engine; it's a configuration that has a zero priority once it moves out onto the open tracks. Everything that moves on road or rail takes precedence. For twenty-four hours our train was jostled on various sidings and tracks and each of us discovered, to our dismay, that we were right back at the same siding where we had boarded the train the day before. The other unbelievable fact was that this train had no dining car or any provision for feeding these several hundred special cadets. Occasionally, when the train would stop and someone would spot a store, several of the men would hop out and buy cartons of candy bars and sell them to the aspiring young airmen. This was my first time to hear the oft repeated expression: "situation normal....all f***ed-up."

We were on this train over three days before reaching San Antonio. By the time we arrived, most of us were sick. No one could believe the air force would treat its recruits in such a manner. Later, we were told that this phase had been handled by the Army; a service with no special feeling for members of the Air Force. As soon as the last man stepped off the train, we were over-powered by screaming sergeants shouting orders. We were herded on the double to various barracks, given innumerable instructions, and informed that our training was just beginning. For the first time we were confronted with the cadet class system. There were the upperclassmen and there were the new recruits . . .us! It didn't take long to learn what R.H.I.P. stands for: (Rank Has Its Privilege). The class system meant that any upperclassman could stop you; ask any question, demand answers and or respect; make you run on the double;

hit "braces"; and a variety of other indignities. Each time an upperclassman confronted one of us, we automatically were compelled to hit a "brace." This brace required the cadet to stand at attention with the shoulders thrown back until the two shoulder blades touched, while the chin had to be pressed against the chest. You had to stand in this position until ordered to fall out. Many of my friends actually fell in a faint when held too long in one of these 'braces."

One of the first things that happened on the positive side was the new summer uniform that we were issued. We were now beginning to look military. Perhaps the most memorable occasion that I can recall about the class system at S.A.A.C.C., pronounced like "Sack" (San Antonio Aviation Cadet Center) was the ordeal we went through when we ate the three meals each day. As underclassmen, we had to eat what was referred to as "square meals." This meant that we sat on the outer two inches of our chair, we passed all of the food to the upperclassmen who sat at each table, we looked only straight ahead, we could not eat until given permission; and when we ate, we had to use our peripheral vision in order to fill our fork. . . and then lift the fork straight up before our face... bring it in to our mouth at a 90° angle. An upperclassman could order you to stand at attention on your chair and recite a poem or perhaps sing your high school or college school song. There was no limit to their imagination for things to harass or annoy an underclassman. They could not touch us, make fun of our religious beliefs, or make remarks about ethnic backgrounds. The Cadet Honor required only truth; and if a Cadet was caught lying or cheating, he was immediately washed out of the Air Corps.

The class system that we had to live by was similar to that incorporated at West Point and Annapolis. The only reprieve we had each day was after the bugler sounded taps at night and until the same damn horn sounded reveille early in the morning. I was one of only a few underclassmen that had to live upstairs on the floor with the upperclassmen; all the rest of the "lowlies" lived on the first floor. Each time I wanted to get to my bed or locker I had to shout out the following from the foot of the stairs:"Sir, Aviation Cadet Lloyd O. Krueger, serial number 16056910 wishes to enter the inner sanctum of the upperclassmen." I then had to wait until someone upstairs yelled, "hit it." You had to take the stairs on the double and if ordered to "freeze," you had to stop and tell what altitude (number of steps up) you were at. At the top you automatically went into a brace until ordered "at ease." It sounds like a lot of "crap" but the purpose was to teach discipline, alertness, how to take orders, how orders are given, quick reaction and response, and above all to overcome shyness. This preparation, which followed us through all of our training, gave each of us a military bearing and pride that most of us carry to this day.

At S.A.A.C.C. we had slightly over a month of being an underclassman before moving on up. On the designated day of this momentous occasion, we went through eight hours of "turn about" where we could work over the upperclassmen before they shipped out. Most of our attention was directed toward the cadets that used their authority with the proper spirit and in keeping with what the class system was designed to do. Those we considered C.S. (Chicken Shit) cadets, we completely ignored, which was a terrific way to let them know that they still had a lot to learn about handling designated power and rank. Hopefully, when and if they became officers, they would lose their "C.S. handle."

The five weeks we spent as upperclassmen went by very rapidly. We were given physical exams and numerous mental tests that would determine which base we would be sent for further training. The physical exam was most thorough. It took most of one week. A great deal of emphasis was placed on eye exams, on our dexterity, and on our reflexes. Some of the devices were very challenging and actually fun. A dozen different doctors checked everything I owned. Another week and a half was devoted to both written and oral tests. All of this would normally have been fun, except that the stakes were very high. If I flunked any part of the physical or mental exams, I would be "washed out." This meant that I might end up in gunnery school, an ordinance branch, mechanics school, as a radio operator, or perhaps back in the regular Army—none of which appealed to me.

Several days after all the results from my tests were tallied, I was called in for the important interview before the review board and given their recommendations and suggestions. I was one of the lucky ones who passed with flying colors. I had qualified for all three flight schools; namely pilot training, navigational training, and bombardier training. I was given the choice of any of the three training courses. I chose pilot training.

On April 23, 1943, I left S.A.A.C.C. for Uvalde, Texas, by Greyhound Bus. There were several bus loads of very happy cadets. This was only a few hour trip; Uvalde is a short distance southwest of San Antonio, but we sang all the way to this pilot primary training school. Uvalde is a small Texas town that just happened to be the home of John Nance Garner, vice president of the United States, under Franklin Delano Roosevelt from 1933 to 1941. Naturally, the field I was assigned to was called "Garner Army Air Base." This field was southeast of town and was like a jewel in the middle of a mesquite-covered prairie. We had palm trees and green grass everywhere. A moment I shall never forget happened

L. O. Krueger
Wausau, WI

AVIATION CADET

P. L. Viviani
Houston, TX
Instructor

F. C. Sweeney
Charleston, W. VA

Geo. Kristy
Henrietta, Ohio

FAIRCHILD PT-19
Soloed - May 20, 1944

just as we arrived and had gotten off the bus. The upperclassmen greeted us and ordered that we line up along a sidewalk on the side of each bus. Immediately, a cadet with high rank charged toward me and put his nose up to mine and started to scream. He was so close and so loud I had difficulty in understanding him. I had the feeling that I had just put a hatchet in his mother's back. Instead, I discovered that the heels of my shoes were touching the grass. I was the example for all. The landscaping at this base was maintained with a great deal of effort by a crew of eight Mexicans and it was a serious matter to get caught stepping on the grass or flowers.

We were assigned to neat single-story barracks with 24 Cadets in each. Once we settled in, the first notice I received was that P.L. Vivani was to be my flight instructor and George Kristy from Henrietta, Ohio, and Fred Sweeney from Charleston, West Virginia, were to be the other Cadets in Flight B. The second thing I realized was that I had gotten sick. With a temperature of 103°, I spent my first week in the infirmary with a serious case of food poisoning. Normally, this would be no great deal, except my group was now involved with intense and accelerated pilot training. About an hour a day was spent at the flight line and approximately 10 hours was spent in classroom or study halls. We had courses on theory of flight, mechanics of the plane, math, weather, link training, radio work,

international morse code, emergency flight and survival courses, military science and physical training. To miss the entire first week was a problem I had to live with. Time waits for no one.

My instructors were all helpful in assisting me to catch up with my buddies; however, with each day so jammed with activities, it was extremely rough. I was given special permission to spend several hours studying in the latrine after lights were out. This helped me catch up with my classwork but my flight time was behind. On May 20th I finally took my solo flight, which lasted for 35 minutes in the single-wing Fairchild PT-19. This was perhaps the greatest thrill I have ever had and it was only marred by the knowledge that I was still a week behind the others in flight time.

On June 14, 1943, I was told to report to the Flight Board at 1400 hours. Along with six other cadets, we were informed that a decision had been reached that would alter our lives. Each of us had qualified for all three flight programs and it was their decision to send us to Navigational School. We were told that actual combat conditions in England had created a dire shortage of first pilots and navigators due to the method of attack on B-17's. The early B-17F models had no chin turrets, thus they permitted the German fighter pilot to approach bombers from the front. As a result, the planes that were shot up and made it back to their bases had a high kill or injury ratio among pilots and navigators. The ranks of first pilots were made up from co-pilots but the navigators had to be shipped from the States. This phase of training required cadets with more skills in mathematics and that was the main reason for being selected. We were told that we could return to pilot training should conditions change, but none of us believed this bull. This was truly a sad day for each to us. I shed tears periodically for the next month each time I let myself dwell on this fate.

On June 16th, we were sent back to San Antonio and the Classification Center to join new classes of cadets. During the next several months we basically sat around while the new group was being classified. We were able to take a few advance courses in math but over all it was really a waste of time. Finally, on August 27, 1943, I received my orders to go to San Marcos, Texas. A bus load of us left San Antonio at 1400 hours and arrived at 1700 hours.

Our training at Navigational School began immediately. It consisted of eight hours minimum of classroom time, six days a week, for the next eighteen weeks. Many weekends were spent on training flights to different southern cities in order to test our navigational skills. I was in the class designated 44-1-8 and suddenly found that I really enjoyed the challenge of navigation as an exact science. Because of my pilot training, instead of being behind, I was probably two weeks ahead of the others. I

**Graduation Day
January 15, 1944
Commissioned 2nd. Lt.**

soon learned that the harder you worked, the more accurate the results. For five months I threw everything I owned into my work; and because of this, I achieved exceptional grades and favorable commendations from many of my instructors. I did not realize it at the moment, but this special effort on my part followed me to England and perhaps was responsible for my being designated Lead Navigator after my ninth mission in combat.

On December 4th I was given a $250.00 allowance to purchase a new officer's uniform. I managed to get a custom job for $256. Man, it was beginning to feel like Christmas. January 15, 1944, was graduation day and I received my commission as a 2nd Lieutenant, a pair of silver navigational wings, and a two-week pass to go home, first time since enlistment!

Immediately after the graduation ceremony, I got a bus to San Antonio and a train to St. Louis, where I spent the night with a friend, and by the 17th I was in Chicago to visit my girlfriend, Norma Ann Schmidt, who was in nurse's training at the time. We spent most of the day together. She had to go back to school and I headed up north to our hometown of Wausau. The plan was that Norma would come home on the weekend so we could be together. On January 23rd, at 0200 hours, we became engaged. This relationship is still going on after 47 years, so the commitment we made that night made her my wife and friend extraordinare. I now had an important reason for making it through the war.

The year and a half since I enlisted had many ups and downs. Although the negative moments outweighed the positive, I have many pleasant memories. These experiences have played an important role in my life because they taught me discipline, patience, perseverance, and the good feeling that achievement brings. As important as these 18 months seemed, my real experiences still lay before me. Looking back now, after these many years, it is obvious that one had to be young and naive to be subjected to this type of accelerated training and be designated a member of a combat crew in a war situation. These were experiences you wouldn't wish on anyone, yet happy that they happened to you.

 Pre-Flight School

When I enlisted as a cadet in the U. S. Airforce, I was aware that I may someday be sent to war against an enemy who had been trained for perhaps a dozen years and who had several years of actual combat exposure. I had no way of knowing just who this opponent might be, a Japanese or a German pilot. It really didn't make much difference, since both of these Axis Powers had veterans developed over many years of aggression.

These men had been instilled with a dynamic militarism that Americans could not possibly comprehend. Their standards and ways of life gave them a determination to play a part in the terrible dream of world conquest. These men, and all their counterparts, were an enemy to be respected and not taken for granted.

In contrast, the young men in the United States had only known freedom—a world where each was inhibited only by such morals as we grew up with and by our own conscience. Each of us had the belief that we had every right to the pursuit of happiness and the right to reach for any goal we believed was within our grasp. History would have to prove whether this dissimilar lifestyle would be able to compete.

The dictators, from both Japan and Germany, believed that Americans were completely incapable of preparing their youth with the necessary discipline for conflict and war. They underrated the desire of a free society to respond to forces that were determined to subjugate a way of life.

Several Pre-flight Schools were set up in various areas of our country shortly after Pearl Harbor. Their purpose was to take on the challenge of converting the youth of this nation into men who would make up our Air Force. These men would be our pilots, navigators, bombardiers, aerial gunners, engineers, radio operators, mechanics, observers, teachers, and all other personal that would be essential for an effective air arm.

When I was shipped out from Nashville, Tennessee, to San Antonio, Texas, I was informed that our group of cadets would start "ground school." This title seemed to be synonymous with my definition of the term "academics," which carried memories of the year that I had spent at the University of Wisconsin as a freshman. These memories had little likeness to what I was about to experience at the S.A.A.C.C. (San Antonio

12 • Pre-Flight School

Aviation Cadet Krueger
Class of 43-J, Flight-B
Garner Field-Uvalde, Texas

Aviation Cadet Center). Each new cadet soon discovered that "mental discipline" should be the key words for a world we were about to enter.

The saunter type of pace that we used between college classrooms was now substituted by military formations and marching in uniform to and from classes. There was little resemblance to my expectations. We would not have to look for "snap" courses, and there would not be "cuts" here. We started our first class each morning at 7 a.m., not 8, 9 or 10 a.m.

Another obvious exception was the lack of coeds. By noon we had attended five different courses without an option to pick electives or courses that had the greatest appeal. The job of all of our instructors was to prepare neophytes for combat. All nonessential activities were eliminated.

Most courses were related or interlocked to have dual purposes. Because of the urgency to quickly prepare each cadet for war, each received training in rapid decisive thinking; not in scholarly contemplation. Mastery of the Morse code and aircraft identification were examples of courses that stressed coordination between the senses and the mind. It was necessary to be alert and develop the ability to make instant decisions to achieve success in these two subjects.

Each cadet was expected to keep their clothes and barracks clean; polish their brass and shoes (the old spit & polish routine); take part in parades and guard duty; find time to study, and prepare for the numerous exams that seemed to occur on a daily basis. This required each individual to maintain a very disciplined schedule that necessitated accounting for every second of each day. The ability to work and think under extreme difficulties prepared each cadet for the myriad of distractions that they might face in actual combat.

Physics, map reading, mathematics, and meteorology prepared the cadet to be pilots, navigators, or bombardiers. The courses themselves were not designed to turn out geniuses or another Einstein. They were constructed to turn out crew members of a flight team with a complete understanding of the basic principals of flight, aerial bombardment, and navigation.

The Cadet Honor System was perhaps the greatest deviation from an ordinary educational system. All tests and exams were unproctored, since each instructor would make it a point to leave the classroom during these moments. Every cadet was honor bound to do his own work without any assistance from notes, glances at other answers, or attempts to converse. Any cadet who cheated on an exam was expected to report himself and to report another cadet caught in the act of cheating. This was immediate cause for dismissal from further training. This honor system developed at Annapolis and West Point was the key to building character in the lives of future officers in the Air Force.

To prepare each cadet for the physical rigors of flying, a very important aspect of the training was physical fitness. Several times a week vigorous training and encouragement in sports conditioned the cadet's body—all in an effort to strengthen the muscles required for flying. No two days in the week were the same. It was planned so that the usual calisthenics did not become boring and dull. The variety of physical training included running through different obstacle courses and cross country trails, archery, tug-of war, boxing, wrestling, medicine ball, tumbling, basketball, volleyball, or judo classes.

Teams were organized at Pre-Flight school for any or all cadets to participate in their favorite sport or sports, thus providing the opportunity for wholesome body-building recreation. I participated in volleyball and softball. I also ran track for the first time in my life, since my high school in Wausau did not offer this sport. To my amazement, I was the fastest runner for the mile at a special track meet. I passed out as I crossed the finish line, got messed up when I fell into the cinders, and I never did find out my time, since I was taken to the infirmary to clean my wounds.

During these weeks we spent at S.A.A.C.C. we were exposed to all of the disciplines necessary to become a member of a flight crew. We took 108 hours of physics, 80 hours of mathematics, 60 hours each for history, English, and geography, 24 hours of civil air regulations. We had courses in meteorology, navigation, military courtesy, hygiene and sanitation, first aid, map reading, aerial photography, and so forth.

In physics, we covered several chapters in our textbook each week. Daily we were exposed to such subjects as heat, mechanics, light, vibration, magnetism, electricity, and radio. All of us had finished high school; some had a year or two of college, and others had graduate degrees. I felt somewhat fortunate with my single year in the Engineering School at the University of Wisconsin. At least my major was in the sciences and my forte was mathematics.

We started the courses in math on square one; we started with simple arithmetic and in less than two months we were into spherical trigonometry. The courses in geography, English, history and meteorology contributed to the required overall knowledge that we were expected to have. The material came fast and furious. Every week our ranks were thinned by individuals who wanted to leave the cadet program because of the fast pace. They just couldn't keep up. It was not how smart you were, but how fast you could assimilate the material for the countless exams. The entire purpose of this type of training was to give each cadet an elementary background in each of the subjects. It also acted like a screening system to find the cadets whose aptitude matched those required to fly.

Just when we believed that we were covering all of the courses known to man, we met with new instructors who exposed us to civil air regulations, flight rules, and aircraft identification, which included all Allied aircraft as well as those of the Japanese and German air forces. We had courses in traffic control, pilot regulations, meteorology, and methods of navigation.

One day, during our second month, we were divided into groups of 16 cadets and taken to the Pressure Chamber. We were going to make a simulated flight in a large cylinder-like cabinet that had a single air-tight door and no windows. It was designed so that the air, and consequently the air pressure, could be reduced. This small chamber duplicated the conditions that we would experience in an airplane at high altitudes.

Each of us entered the room while stripped down to our waist. A medical officer checked us over and stood by, should his services be required. We were each given a pad of paper and a pencil and were instructed to periodically write a specific sentence or word. None of us wore oxygen masks, though they were mounted on the wall behind each cadet. As the air was expelled, we were being deprived of oxygen. Later, we learned that our handwriting turned into illegible scrawls as the simulated altitude approached 10,000 feet. One by one we physically passed out. Instructors immediately put each cadet on oxygen and within seconds each cadet responded. We learned the meaning of the word "anoxia," and we learned that the more we were deprived of this important element, the more euphoric we became. This was a lesson that we would need on every flight that we took where our altitude exceeded 10,000 ft. It was also important to realize that, while we were attending all of these classes, studying, and taking required exams, each cadet was operating under the class system. For the first month, you were classified as an underclassman and during the second month you became an upperclassman. This fact is mentioned to point out that during our stay at S.A.A.C.C. that we were subjected to all forms of hazing and that we had to march to class, to drill fields, to mess, and to get our weekly haircut. In addition, we had to hit braces, recite poetry, sing school songs, and anything else that someone had devised to occupy our every minute.

In the morning, usually before the sun was up, we were awaken by the sound of a bugle calling us for reveille. This meant flying off our cot, getting dressed in uniform, dashing out in front of our barracks, getting into formation, and answering to roll call. After a dismissal order we then raced back into the barracks, shaved and showered, made our bed in a prescribed way, folded all of our clothing in multiples of 4" because they would be exposed on open shelves, and cleaned up our own area. Periodically, along with several other cadets we would have the responsibility of cleaning the aisles and the latrine. The top blanket on the bed had to be pulled tight enough so that a coin would bounce into the air.

Each Saturday the barracks was inspected by a contingent of officers who checked each cadet and his domain. This inspection was conducted with white gloves so that a small amount of dust could be ascertained. Any infraction meant a demerit. For every demerit over five each week, the cadet had to drill or march on the parade grounds for an hour as punishment. Late Saturday morning all of the cadets marched to the huge parade field. Since there were 10,000 cadets at the S.A.A.C.C., it made quite a show, with marching formations being led from every corner of the base. Each barracks had its own flag, and the leaders and each barracks marched as a unit to a prescribed place on the parade ground. We were dressed in our finest—complete with white gloves. If you moved a finger to touch an itch on you nose or to stop a bead of sweat, an officer would reprimand you instantly. To get the men on the field, inspect all ranks, and finally be dismissed took several hours. It was just another ordeal.

When I first arrived at Pre-Flight School, I was told, for example, that I had ten minutes to leave a formation returning from P.T.(physical training); go into the barracks and shower; change into a clean uniform; put all of my clothes away; run out of the barracks and get into a formation ready to march to a classroom. I believed this to be an impossible task. Within two days, all cadets were doing this very thing. We soon learned how to do the difficult and found that the impossible only took a little longer.

I had arrived at the San Antonio Pre-Flight School on April 23, 1943, and I actually finished my training in the middle of the following June, two months later. The last week was spent on written and oral exams that covered the many subjects that we had been exposed to. We each knew that the hour of truth would arrive at the end of these exams. Our ranks had been thinned over the past eight weeks by individuals who had lost their desire to fly; who could not stand the class system and all that it implied; who were falling behind in class work; who flunked too many courses; or who were caught cheating.

On June 15th each cadet was scheduled to meet with a board of review whose purpose was to report on each cadet's status. They would make an evaluation and then state their recommendations on our future. There were really only four routes each of us could go. We could be assigned to pilot training; navigational training; bombardier training; or be eliminated entirely from officer's training. The later meant that you might go to gunnery school; go for training as a mechanic; go to radio school; or go to

a variety of other fields related to the Air Force, usually with a noncommissioned rank.

The few minutes I stood at attention before the four officers on the review board seemed like an hour. With some formality I was informed that I had qualified for all three training centers; namely, pilot, navigational, and bombardier flight schools. I could have my pick. With little hesitation, I chose pilot training. I was then informed that tomorrow, June 16th, I would be shipped to Uvalde, Texas, in the new Class of 43-J. Here I would start an entirely new life and receive very specialized training.

This perhaps was my second most memorable and pleasurable moment in the Air Force. My first choice would come sometime later at Primary Pilot Training when I got the opportunity to take-off in a plane and solo for the first time. The type of training and exposure we had received during these two months, nearly 1500 hours of elapsed time, gave all of the survivors something that words alone can not describe. This same technique for discipline and training would follow us through flight training and up to the moment we would receive our commission as an officer in the U. S. Air Force.

These same two months, that the government set aside as Pre Flight, each cadet was taken as a piece of putty and molded them into a disciplined candidate as a flight officer. It was a concentrated period in each of our lives that could never be forgotten. Each gained almost instant maturity.

 Deutschland and Beyond

It was Wednesday night, May 11, 1944, while at the 95th Bomb Group Officers Club, that we received the notice that the bar would be closed in ten minutes: the Red Flag had been raised. This signaled to all on the base that tomorrow's weather appeared good enough to schedule a mission. As Lt. Ray Weakland rushed in to pick up a drink and beat the deadline, he informed me that my name was on the board to fly with Lt. Snowden's crew. "Weak" was the bombardier on my crew and was awaiting the word that the crew of HAARD LUCK would be called up for their first mission. I had been pulled away from my crew and had flown with Lt. Woods two days ago for my first trip over Europe.

On May 9th, I had flown to Laon Athies, France. We bombed an airfield just west of Paris and experienced very little flak and no enemy fighters. This first mission turned out to be both a short trip and one with a minimum of risk. I instantly came to the false conclusion that fighting against the German war machine was going to be "duck soup." Was I in for some surprises?

I walked back to the barracks with "Waddy" and "Weak" with some mixed emotions. I was excited that I was going on my second mission just three days after my first one, but I felt sorry for the members of my own crew, since they had yet to experience combat and to begin their tour of duty. It turned out that all of us in the crew of "HAARD LUCK" would fly our first mission together on the 13th of May. Tonight, though, none of us knew this and we walked in silence.

I hit the sack by 2130 hours, knowing that I would get a wake-up nudge by 0300 hr., the middle of the night. As I was "flaked" out on my cot, I tried to talk myself into falling asleep, but the excitement of tomorrow kept me awake for hours. I tried to guess where we were going; what type of target it might be; if our fighter escort could be with us the entire trip; if German fighters would come to meet us; how intense the flak might be over the target. These were all details that I had no way of knowing. At the other end of the barracks, several fellows were playing poker, while others were writing letters or just taking part in a bull session. All kept their voices down in consideration for the guys who had

HOME AWAY FROM HOME

TYPICAL BARRACKS SCENE

to fly tomorrow. I have no idea about how much sleep I managed to get, except to know that I was awaken by the rays from a flashlight shining on my heavy eyelids and a gentle voice informing me that it was time to hit the deck.

As I started to get dressed by the dim light escaping from the distant wash room, I could see Cobb, "Waddy," and "Weak" sleeping. Suddenly, I felt lonesome. My first mission was flown with Lt. Wood and his crew, and today I would fly with still another group of fellows I had never met. These were things that I had never counted on. I believed that we would all stick together through our entire tour of duty, just as we had trained for, but the darkness of this lonely barracks was only interrupted by the many different snores.

Only a handful of us left the barracks for the trip to the mess hall in the cold, damp morning air. There would be no laughing or joking around. Each of us shuffled off in the dark, each with our own thoughts. The mess hall was also dimly lit with only a skeleton crew on hand to feed the sleepy, groggy flyers. Everyone seemed to move about in slow motion and none felt like eating at this ungodly hour. Yet, we all knew that if we were lucky enough to return from the mission that it would be late in the day before we saw food again.

The Briefing Hut was only a short haul away from the mess hall. All of the zombies started to come to life with the anticipation of knowing the where and type of target that headquarters had planned for this day. Each of us had to report to an officer at the guarded briefing room door. It was important to know if each member of each scheduled crew was present and also important to protect the secrecy of the upcoming mission.

The room was long, taking up nearly all of the space in a large Nisson Quonset Hut. The first thing that I noticed was the thick smoke from the hundreds of burning cigarettes and cigars. The small 60 watt light bulbs looked like little yellow fuzz balls as they tried to penetrate the polluted air. The brightest lights were at the far end of the room and were directed to the end wall that held a huge map of Europe. On this map were tacks from which a colored string had wend its way from our base at Horham, England, across the Channel to a target in Belgium, the Netherlands, France or perhaps, Germany. This map was always covered with a drape or curtain when I entered this room. Many guys kept going out for "nervous pees" as the excitement built.

This was only my second mission so I still was learning what to expect and sort of absorbing the nervous tension all around me. I soon became aware of many different odors. The most dominant fragrance that permeated the smoky air was the smell of sweat. Each of us was dressed in a heavy flying suit and boots for the sub-zero temperatures that we knew

22 • Deutschland and Beyond

Control tower along west perimeter

"Shackling-up" and preparing 500 pound bombs for our mission to Berlin. Eight of these bombs are pulled up into the bomb bay and armed.

we would have to withstand. We had all the zippers and buttons opened to withstand the heat in this unventilated room. We looked squabby and unkept. We did not live up to the Hollywood version of the image of what a combat crew about to take off on a mission should look like. Everyone in this stuffy setting had only one thing on their mind....where to?

The room filled from front to back. We all knew that this was no church nor school classroom. We all wanted to be where we could see and hear. But somehow, today, there seemed to be an unusual amount of anxiety. The veteran crews sensed this was going to be a long haul, deep into Germany. Being a beginner, I had my ears tuned into six or seven different conversations, trying to pick up as much info as possible. It was impossible to make sense from all this nervous chatter and unrest. We were only moments away from the exposed map and the truth of the day.

At the prescribed minute, the Commanding Officer, Col. Carl Truesdell, Jr. entered the room and all popped to attention and a contrasting stillness filled the space. This would be the Colonel's first briefing as the new C.O. of the 95th Bombardment Group. He had just replaced Co. Chester P. Gilger, who was moved upstairs. Col. Truesdell had picked a difficult mission to begin his career as a commanding officer.

When the curtain was pulled back to the right, it became obvious that this would be one of the longest raids in the war to this point. The string ran out from Horham, our bomber base, across the Channel to our European Landfall at Vlissingen, Netherlands, southwest of Rotterdam. From there it bent its way between Cologne and Frankfurt, Germany, and continued on to a place they said was Brux, Czechoslovakia, a town about 50 miles northwest of Prague.

The moans and groans were enough to clear the air. No one seemed pleased. Col. Truesdell pulled the cigar from his mouth and stated, "Today's target is part of a maximum effort by the American 8th Air Force. Two thousand heavy bombers and fighters will fly out to hit five major synthetic oil plants, four in the Leipzig area of Germany and one at Brux. Targets to be attacked in Germany will include oil plants at Merseburg, Bohlen, Lutzkendorf and Zeitz. Our target is over 600 miles in a direct line from our base and we all know that we never took the shortest route. We also know that our fighter escort could only help us on the first half of this mission. The rest of the time we would be on our own. Gentlemen, this is the type of target that you don't want to go back to—do a good job this day. Good luck."

You could have heard a pin drop. The map before us told each person in the room that the hours ahead would not be easy. We did not have too much time to dwell on our thoughts because Major Clyde Bingham told us what to expect at the target area. The oil plant was very important to the German war effort and therefore had crack German anti-aircraft crews. We could expect intense flak at our target. Because of the length of this mission, we all knew we would have to weather half of our trip without fighter plane escort. Since this period of the war was before the addition of droppable wing tanks for our fighters, their range was approximately 300 miles from England. Needless to say, there was a great deal of apprehension this morning in the briefing rooms in the many Groups scattered throughout eastern England.

Operations gave us details for taxing and take-off times, for the field order given for the time of assembling, and for the time we could expect to rendezvous with our supporting fighters. The weather officer informed us that the weather over most of Europe would be fair and that no clouds should obscure the target area.

As a navigator, I had to stay behind while the rest of the crew went to their various hardstands and their respective planes. All navigators were given additional detailed information regarding the exact route to target and return. We had specific coordinates to hit at specific times in order to rendezvous with other groups and other wings who would join us on this venture. Our route was laid out to avoid as much flak as possible and to also deceive the Germans as to just what targets were to be hit. We were given expected wind velocity and direction for critical altitudes, and alternate targets were discussed in case of problems at the primary target. With all of our maps and gear, each navigator was trucked to a hardstand around the perimeter of the field in order to join their respective crews. This morning I was to meet and fly with Charlie Snowden's crew for the first time.

At approximately 0600 we boarded our plane, which happen be old No. 297334, "HAARD LUCK," which was the plane we flew from the States. By 0610 hr. a flare was fired from the control tower and the first B-17 slowly started to taxi. Soon all 42 B-17's were moving around both sides of the 3.5 mile perimeter. The planes were lined up, one behind the other, waiting for the signal to take to the air and get this long day underway. Another flare was fired and Col. Dave McKnight and the lead crew headed down runway 25, followed by the other planes at 30 second intervals. This morning the 200 foot wide runway seemed especially narrow and very bumping. We lumbered down and seemed to pick up just enough air speed to pull this clumsy bird into the cold morning air. We were on our way.

Today, the weather over eastern England was better than usual. We had a 10 mile visibility with only scattered clouds with which to contend. We headed and climbed in a northeasterly direction toward Radio Buncher No. 8, which is near Great Yarmouth on the coast. All 42 planes circled until each could get into their assigned position in the formation of the 95th B.G. A total of 6 B-17s dropped out of formation and returned to base because of equipment troubles. Plane No. 23263 reported an oil leak at take-off and didn't even climb to altitude. Lt. Jacobsen reported an engine failure and pulled away. As we approached Buncher No. 8, Lt. Bertram and Lt. Wyrick both had their No. 3 engine fail. Lts. Pinas and Doherty discovered oxygen leaks and had to return to the base. This was not a good start and it required some adjustment in the entire formation. So much for detailed planning. Because of the length of this particular mission, this was no time to take unnecessary chances with malfunctioning equipment. The 95th was down to 36 planes from the four Squadrons; namely, the 334th, 335th, 336th and the 412th.

At 0720 hr. our Group headed southwest toward Splasher 6, near Thorpe. Along the way we picked up the 100th Bomb Group and the 390th Bomb Group to make up the 13th Wing. At 0742 hr. we were over Splasher 7 at 25,000 feet. The 4th and 13th Wings joined in trail behind the 45th Wing. Splasher 7 was near Colchester, only a ten minute flight to Felixstowe, our departure point from England. The 3rd Division was on its way with over 300 heavy bombers...what a sight. Other Divisions would visit the area around Leipzig to hit the other four synthetic oil plants.

At 0810 hr. we reached our landfall point at Vlissingen, Netherlands. Some of our "little friends" have now joined us. Our escort was made up primarily of P-47s and P-38s. What a comforting sight. As we crossed over the Ruhr Valley, we picked up some flak. This was to be expected since this is the heart of the Nazi industrial area and is the most heavily fortified with both flak guns and fighter planes.

Shortly after our fighter escort broke off and dropped down to "the deck" to seek out targets on their return to their bases, we heard the first reports of German fighters. They had been waiting for this moment. The first Groups hit were up ahead of us, just north of Frankfurt, Germany. We could see several hundred fighters in various size formations. They would peel off and attack the B-17s from all directions. They looked like a swarm of bees around a disturbed hive. At 0952 the 95th, the 100th, and the 390th got their chance. With shaky legs I manned my right 50 cal. machine gun and began firing at enemy aircraft streaking past at closing speeds of 500 mph. This was the very first time I had fired a gun in combat and it turned out to be the last. My floor was covered with empty shell casings; I was slipping and sliding over these rolling pieces of brass, and the nose was filled with smoke and the smell of powder. The noise was deafening. I previously had only fired a gun for a few bursts over the Channel on one of our practice missions. This was different. I found out later that you should only fire off 8 second bursts so the gun would not over heat. I ruined the gun when the barrel bent out of shape and a shell got jammed in the breach. I could not get it fixed. My other

26 • Deutschland and Beyond

The streaming contrails of the 3rd Air Division—B-17's heading out

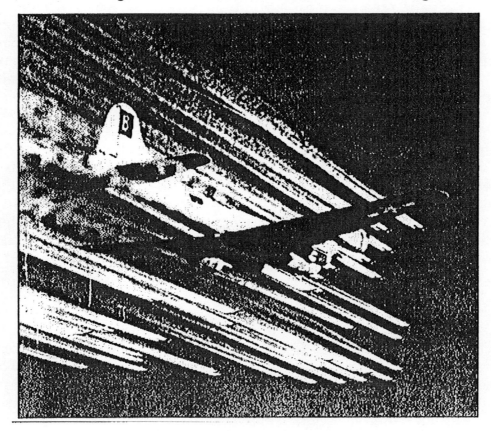
95th Bomb Group crossing the channel.
Flying tight formation is essential—contrails occurred at only certain altitudes

gun was useless because of the narrow angle of swing and the visibility. Planes went by so fast there was no time to react. Gunners were screaming that fighters were approaching our formation from all directions: "12 o'clock high; another is coming in at 11 o'clock low; here one comes at 3 o'clock level; four more are approaching at 6 o'clock low; here's one—9 o'clock high." It was impossible to use this type of information in a coherent way, especially with the way my guns were designed. Each man had to track the one plane that seemed to be the most threatening to him. In order to be successful with this type of combat, you always had to aim between the incoming fighter and your own plane; figuring this out was not always easy. Sometimes it required luck.

The German fighters had the same problems with the constantly changing positions of their target and the commotion of the battle.

Planes were falling out of formation; some were dropping like autumn leaves; others were diving in a lazy arc toward the earth; and others exploded into a ball of fire. German fighters left a trail of smoke as they streamed toward the ground. By the time we were attacked by groups of fighters, the B-17s from the Groups ahead of us were now hitting the ground with explosive impact. Things were happening so fast. There was too much to absorb. There were fighters trying to knock you out of their air-space; six gunners and a bombardier were each yelling into their mikes; the approach of enemy planes; the normal roar of four engines cranking out over 4000 horsepower plus the chatter of ten or twelve 50 caliber machine guns firing at the same time and the smell and smoke from hundreds of fired shells. All these elements going on simultaneously, made you believe that you were in the middle of a wild and senseless dream. Then as fast as this horrible moment began, it ended. The noises that remained were conditions that you had grown used to. Some of these attacks lasted only minutes, but they seemed like eternities.

The 95th Bomb Group had always had an excellent record of flying a tight and almost picture perfect formation. This close formation sometimes discouraged the Germans from hitting our Group, and instead they would pick on a loose flying unit ahead or behind it. Today, the Germans were attacking all Groups, including the 95th. Our planes were sustaining damage but so far, all 36 B-17s were holding their position. Suddenly Lt. Yablonski's plane veered off to the left and pulled down and away from the formation. The order had been given to abandon ship and two parachutes were counted by our gunners. Shortly thereafter, the plane exploded in a ball of fire and pieces of the B-17 were thrown in all directions before gravity moved them downward. We learned later that the two men who were lucky to escape this falling airplane were Sgts. Harbeck and Dimayo, the radio operator and the ball turret gunner. They were captured by the Germans and spent the rest of the war as POWs.

The remaining crew members, Yablonski, Corrigan, Madigan, Hume, Lyons and Smith, were all killed instantly in the explosion.

Minutes after we had lost one of our own, the Germans broke away from our Group. For whatever reason they turned away—lack of fuel or the losses inflicted by us—each of us was elated. The temperature this day at 27,000 ft. altitude was probably 40 degrees below zero. But this did not stop the beads of sweat from running down your spine. Suddenly, the wet body reacted to the reality of the sub-normal temperature. Shaky legs became stable and conversation over the intercom became somewhat normal. We had made it through this living hell and we were still only halfway to our target. Normal duties helped to put this mad experience into the back of our minds, and we began functioning as though this was only a terrible dream.

My first major experience with this phase of combat helped to straighten out some of the many problems that I had with religion and my total belief in God (as I was taught by my Sunday School teachers and the minister of the church to which I had belonged). I had a very confused feeling between what I had been taught and what I had actually experienced in my young life. I did not know who or what God was. I could not relate to a God who was both kind and caring, and also one who would permit acts of violence and suffering. I had been taught that man was created in the image of God. This to me meant that God must have some of the characteristics of man. This thought would add confusion to my feelings for this type of God or his relation to man. The other problem I had was handling the idea that a person's soul would go to heaven or hell, depending on the type of life one led. I knew that no doctor could perform an autopsy on a human body and retrieve a soul, and I knew that no astronomer or geologist could pinpoint a heaven or a hell. My summation of these facts indicated that we had "nothing going nowhere"; a very confusing thesis that only added to my already confused mind.

My experiences, this 12th day of May, 1944, gave me an insight as to who or what my God was. During the heat of the air battle, I knew that as close as I was to the bombardier and my two pilots, none of these men could do anything to protect me or to remove the emanate dangers. I could reach out and with little effort touch any of these men, yet I could do nothing that would truly protect them. At this moment, I knew that the only source of comfort was the thought of a God. Yes, I did pray on this and several other similar missions, and the fact that I am sitting here with my typewriter would indicate that perhaps these prayers were answered. I arrived at the belief that there surely was a God, but my God was not earthly nor resembled man in any way. My God was a power, a precise force, a force that controlled order and laws of nature. These laws, such as the law of averages and the laws of probability, could be explained; they could predict results both in the past and in the future, and they would be constant. I knew that this German fighter pilot or the German gunner that controlled the 88mm anti-aircraft gun throwing up flak believed in a God and also believed that their cause was as just as mine. In the order of things, each person's time will come when one of these laws determines it. Yes, I suppose I could be called a Fatalist, a believer that all events are determined by necessity, or fate.

At 1134 hr. the 95th reached the I.P.Point near the town of Chomutov, Czechoslovakia. We turned on a heading of 52° for our eight minute run to the target. We were immediately greeted with a wall of flak. Each burst resembled an inverted "Y" that was created in fuzzy black smoke and that appeared to be about ten foot high, with all legs of this figure about a foot wide. Usually, if you saw a single burst, it was soon to be followed by four or five additional ones. I suspect that they inserted clips into their gun with four or five 88mm shells. By the time we could see these ominous shapes of smoke, the shell had already burst into thousands of tiny pieces of shrapnel, each spinning into space and searching for something to pierce or tear apart. Sometimes larger chunks would be thrown out in our direction. Anyone of these pieces could easily pass through the thin aluminum skin of our B-17 and still have the force to penetrate the body or some vital part of the plane itself. The flak we were facing today was a new experience and one that we all learned to live with. We could not fight back at it nor in anyway stop it.

The only challenge we could extend to the gunners of the enemy was to throw out chaff. Chaff was small pieces of aluminum foil that was cut up and bundled. Our gunners would throw this out of the B-17 and let it drift slowly earthward. This chaff could be picked up on the German radar that determined the altitude of the bomber formations and that set the timing of when these 88mm shells would explode. Chaff sometimes would lower the bursts, therefore, helping the high squadrons and perhaps hurting the lower ones. Once you turn into the target from the I. P. Point, the formation can not carry out evasive action or deviate whatsoever from the course. It is during this straight run that the lead bombardier is getting the target set in his Norden Bomb Sight and is determining just when to release these eggs of destruction. The German gunners knew that these formations of planes would be on a constant heading, so it was not hard for them to place walls of flak along the entire length of our bomb run.

Distant burst of flak would throw shrapnel against the plane and made it sound like we were flying through a storm in which the hail stones were the size of golf balls. A direct hit could cut a plane in two or take off a wing. If it hit the gas tanks it would cause an instant explosion. A small piece of flak that hit an engine could immediately put it out of operation. One tiny piece of flak, the size of a little finger nail, could tear an arm off or rip a hole in the flesh that you could put your fist into. This was a new and different kind of hell. It caused new fears and created different kinds of emotions. There is no way to explain the true experience of flying for eight or ten minutes through flak—you would have to live these moments yourself.

At 1140 hrs. the lead ship had opened their bomb bay doors and the other 34 planes followed suit. At 1142 hrs. bombs were away. Immediately, each plane lurched upward, relieved of the 4,000 pound load it was carrying. As we looked down from our 27,000 ft. platform, we could see the bombs exploding from the Groups ahead. Black thick smoke was reaching skyward, bent only slightly by the prevailing winds. The few scattered clouds allowed us to see our target clearly and to see the results of the horrendous effort we had put forth. Many flyers would die from both sides of the war today, and one could only hope that the determination would help to bring this senseless war to an earlier climax.

Immediately after the bombs were away, the 95th Group turned to an approximate heading of due north to clear the obvious flak pattern. At 1145 hr. the entire Group turned to its predetermined heading that was almost due west. It was a heading that would take us back to England and to a respite from the enemy. A check of all of the stations on our plane found no one had been hit and there appeared to be no major damage to the plane despite the several dozen holes that were counted. I picked up four pieces of flak for the collection that I was now starting. Several planes in our formation had one or two engines out, and they were flying with their propellers feathered. Each of these planes was managing to hold its position in the formation. Sometimes, if you can not maintain altitude or airspeed, it becomes necessary to leave the formation and try and make it back to your base on your own. If German fighters find one of these cripples, they immediately take advantage of the situation and attack. The outcome is usually in favor of the fighters. The greatest protection for each plane is within the tight formation of the entire Group and within its approximate four hundred 50 cal. machine guns. Below and away from our Group you could spot several B-17s limping home. Our hope for our fellow flyers was that they could get picked up by some of our "little friends" and escorted back. It would be at least an hour before they could expect this kind of help because of the length of today's mission.

Near Giessen, Germany, we were again hit by fighters. The Group ahead lost several planes and we counted nearly 30 parachutes, both from bombers and from German fighter planes. Nearly forty FW190s and ME 109s hit us just as our American fighters were arriving. We had lucked out. We witnessed a few dog fights, and in seconds the enemy vanished. The sky was ours again. Our success depended so much on the help from our "little brothers." It was only a matter of a short time before new technology permitted our P-47, P-38, and especially the P-51 to escort us to all targets. They couldn't help us with flak, but they certainly made the German fighter plane think twice before slamming into the heavy bombers.

As we crossed over the Ruhr Valley, we again picked up a small amount of enemy flak. This was of no consequence compared to the flak that we had witnessed at Brux. The target had been visible for over one-half hour because the smoke from the oil fires had nearly reached our altitude of 27,000 ft. It was intensely black as I would guess an oil fire would suggest. This was a most comforting sight to bring home. By 1624 hr. we could see the Channel; and in a moment, we left the continent near Zeebugge, Holland. By 1658 hr. we had crossed the narrow Channel, had dropped to an altitude of only a few thousand feet, and flew over Aldeburgh, England, only a few minutes away from our Base at Horham.

The planes with battle damage or wounded men were permitted to peel off from the formation and land first. There were 11 of our B-17s in this classification. The 95th was one of the fortunate Groups. It only lost one plane and several wounded airmen. I do not know the total cost of this major effort to hit the five synthetic oil plants, but a report that was printed in the *Stars & Stripes* news service stated the following: "German broadcast described the raid as one of the most widespread, most dramatic, but also most costly operations ever carried out." They went on to report: "Maj. Freytag, air correspondent of the German News Agency, said that 16 U.S. four engine bombers crashed within a few minutes in the Moselle area alone."

By 1715 hr. Lt. Snowden, his crew, and "HAARD LUCK" touched down and were home. Now, it was time to turn our plane over to the Ground Crew, to clean out the shell casings, to repair all damage, and to patch up the many holes in our beautiful lady's skin.

A truck was waiting to take the tired but certainly grateful crew to be interrogated. We were offered a shot of brandy and asked to unwind. A specially trained officer asked each person his rendition of the entire mission. Each person's version was slightly different, but of course, we each had a different seat during this spectacle. The navigators kept notes and were expected to be the most factual. Much had to be jotted down after the fact. There were times when it was impossible to calmly record the events as they were happening. Also, it was not possible to translate the emotions that exploded at certain times. Our interrogator understood these things. Mission number 2 was now recorded, and I arrived back at my barracks just in time to go to supper with my friends. We had been in the air over nine hours and had flown over 1,300 miles. This was to be my longest flight both in miles traveled and duration. Unfortunately, it was not to be my most hectic. That had to wait for another day.

While we were eating supper, I was informed that I was to fly tomorrow; this time I was flying with my original crew on their first mission. As tired as my body felt, I can honestly say that I welcomed this news. In the morning we were going to Osnabruck, Germany. I remember that when I was relating all that had happen on this raid to Brux, Czechoslovakia, to my friends, it felt like it had happened to someone else, except I knew all of the details. I look back now and realize that my mind did not dwell on the death of Lt. Yablonski and his crew, or of the many planes I saw fall from the sky. War was becoming an athletic event like football, where you didn't hate your opponent, where you tried to advance your cause knowing that the other side was going to try and stop you. You learned to take your licks but you took satisfaction in dishing then out. This attitude, perhaps, was to my benefit since no sense can be made of war and all of the reasons human beings try to destroy one another. If we have to have war, then it has to be for the young. Yet, all wars should be fought by the statesmen who so eagerly get their countries involved.

 In Retrospect

In life many things can be broken down to their least common denominator. In combat for instance, you are either a hero or a coward. Wrong. Nearly all our precious moments are periods of various shades of grey. There are brief periods when things tend to be sharper and more precise, and there are those times when many things appear out of focus and very fuzzy.

One of those brief, dull grey periods in my life has bothered me for forty-five years, and it is only now that I believe that I understand and can put it into proper perspective. The events that I relate in the following chapters are taken from diary notes, memory recall, conversations with crew members, and other information that came in over the years.

Shortly after graduation from San Marcos, Texas Navigational Training School, I received my commission as an officer in the United States Air Force and I was assigned to a base at Alexandria, Louisiana. It was here, in February of 1944, that I joined a ten man crew that would be sent off into combat. At this moment in my life, my chief concern was that the war would be over before I got into it. This was a typical attitude expressed by many young and certainly foolish friends of mine.

It was with great excitement that I anticipated meeting each of the other nine members of the crew. I am sure each of these ten young men had a great deal of apprehension about the other members of this important team. Since I am eternally optimistic, I scrutinized each individual very quickly and immediately felt that we were going to have the best B-17 crew in the 8th Air Force.

Our first pilot was a six-foot four inch, red-headed Irishman from Crown Point, Indiana, who had an air of total competency. This story is really about Frank Cobb and about the events that affected each of the crew member's lives.

The co-pilot, Dan "Waddy" Waddell from Hendersonville, North Carolina, was the epitome of a true southerner. He had a slow determined drawl that could take him five minutes just to say "what ya awl doing." We became instant friends and remain friends to this day. The navigator for this auspicious crew was yours truly, a young eager beaver with hay

34 • In Retrospect

seeds in his hair from Wausau, Wisconsin. He felt that he was well trained and couldn't possibly imagine a situation that didn't have an immediate solution. His only uncertainty at this first meeting was that the other strangers might not feel as comfortable with him as he did with them.

The bombardier was Ray "Weak" Weakland from Barnesboro, Pennsylvania He was married, as were Cobb and Waddell, except he had to leave his wife behind because she was pregnant and about to give birth to their first child. This was later to have a drastic effect on Weakland. The above four were each Second Lieutenants and were the officers of our crew.

The six gunners that made up the remainder of the team were all sergeants except one, a PFC; and they all appeared to me much younger than their officers. This was an unusual observation since, I was only twenty-two at the time and probably not any older than some or most of the gunners. The engineer was Sgt. James "Jim" Eavenson, from Waynesville, North Carolina, and he was extremely competent. Jim was the oldest of the gunners and the one who rode herd on the other five. Sgt. Quetin "Newsy" Newswanger from Quarrville, Pennsylvania, was our radio operator and without any doubt, the talkative one of the crew. Sgt. Frank Tomsey, referred to as Tomsey, was from Endicott, New York. He was the smallest member of the crew and had been relegated to the position of ball turret gunner for obvious reasons. Sgt. James "Jim" Argyrakis from Chicago rode in the tail and was our tail gunner. Sgt. I. J. Ellender from Sulphur, Louisiana, and PFC Herman "Hank" Fleet from Houston, Texas, were our two waist gunners and rounded out the entire crew of ten.

Ten young men from eight different states, and each so different in every way. We were brought together by fate to act as one. The predetermined course of events is often conceived as a resistless power. Each of us in the B-17 crew had to learn to accept this fact of fate; and in our own way, had to learn to understand it.

It is important to relate all of the above information in order to give real meaning to the simple term "crew." However, this story is about Cobb, the First Pilot of this young but eager crew. When we we were assembled in Alexandria, we had several practice missions over the Gulf of Mexico, which was a new and exciting experience. We flew our first B-17, the Flying Fortress manufactured by the Boeing Company. It was a Model F, without a chin gun turret, but every inch a bomber. Each member had a chance to practice his skills and to get used to the piece of equipment that would help us be a part of ending the war.

Grand Island, Nebraska, was our next assigned base. It was here that we were given additional training to become more proficient. At this time we were presented with a new shiny B-17G Bomber, which was the plane most responsible for having the war in Europe end on a successful note for the Allies.

We took several flights with our "new baby" for me, as navigator, to calibrate the directional and altitude instruments. This was a boring, but an essential procedure. It is important to note and understand that each member of the crew performed as well as could be expected, especially Lt. Cobb. He was cocky, almost to the point of being arrogant, but he showed leadership qualities to all in his presence. He did not drink, smoke, or gamble. This immediately caused his isolation from other officers, and especially from Waddy and myself. These negative habits had a therapeutic effect and each provided outlets for pent up emotions.

Cobb, as I have noted, was 6'4" tall with a build and physique that was impossible not to notice. He always wore a flaming red scarf. This scarf was wrapped around his neck and was long enough that nearly three feet of material fell down the front and the back of his A-2 leather flight jacket. When he walked it was always at a fast pace with long and confident strides. With my bottom built so close to the ground, it was impossible for me to keep up with him. As he strode around the base, his red scarf usually took on a horizontal position as it waved behind him. My memory of this scene of Frank Cobb dashing about is one of a giant "Snoopy" coming alive.

The orders finally came to send us off to combat, ready or not. The first leg of our journey to England would be from Grand Island to Bangor, Maine. Cobb requested that I work out a heading to Crown Point, Indiana, his hometown, since it was not too far from our dictated course. About ten miles from his home, we let down to tree top level and proceeded to buzz his old neighborhood from several different directions. The four engines on our new B-17 were intentionally out of synchronization in order to add to the noise and effect. Frank must have telephoned his mother because she was in the backyard waving a white bed sheet frantically as most of her neighbors cheered her on. We found out later that many windows had been broken or cracked because of this last hurrah by our Flying Fortress.

The next leg on this long journey was from Bangor to Goosebay, Labordor, and it was the first time many of our crew had ever left the United States. Some miles from the base, Cobb was informed by the control tower that the main runway had a water hazard on the left side and that he should land right of center. Since the runway was nearly 200 ft. wide, this would be no problem. For some reason Cobb brought the plane down left of center and managed to land in the water, kicking up ice chunks that caused some plane damage. Because of the location of Goosebay, snow had accumulated to the point where snow was banked over 20 feet high along the runway and around the parking revetments.

These hazards might of been the reason for Cobb not hugging the right side. In any case, after we parked the plane, I proceeded to climb a ladder so that I could put the canvas cover over the pitot tube protruding from the left side of the nose. I did not know that this pitot tube had a heater in it and grabbed the tube to pull myself up the final step on the ladder. Someone had left the heater switch on and I discovered, much to my consternation, that the pitot tube was red hot. All of the cords in my left hand immediately contracted, pulling my fingers into a fist. Obviously, the pain was something I did not want or need at this time. Because of damage to the plane, it had to be repaired. Thus, my injury was not the sole reason for the several days delay in reaching our destination. It was imperative that I have the use of both hands in order to use a sextant, a complex instrument to shoot and determine the altitude of the stars.

When the repairs had been made to our plane, the doctors bandaged each of my five fingers separately, making it nearly impossible to function with this hand. We were sent on our way to the next stop, Reykjavik, Iceland. Once we took off, I had Lt. Weakland rebandage my hand so the thumb was free and the other fingers were bound together. We had enough bandages left over for several other catastrophes, which fortunately did not occur. Enroute to Iceland, the entire crew had the opportunity to witness a most spectacular display of Northern Lights, the Aurora Borealis. This luminous phenomenon had flashes of light undulating across the heavens. The intercom became flooded with questions about what was happening. I was able to explain that it was a natural occurrence and not to be alarmed. This memory will stay with me as long as I live.

Iceland is a sovereign state with allegiance to Denmark. The flight to this remote island required flying over vast stretches of ocean and to do it at night. The friendliness of the northern lights belies the real problems of navigating in this part of the world. All our compasses in the airplane become worthless due to the magnetic north pole—the extreme variation on readings and the electrical disturbances caused in the atmosphere. This was my moment of truth as the navigator. My job was to accurately locate us on earth and to ascertain a true course to our destination. We experienced winds of excessive velocities that came from irreconcilable directions; all this made my job very challenging.

These many unusual forces acting on the plane made Lt. Cobb most uneasy. His compass read that we were heading south down the middle of the Atlantic, which was a direction that could only have one outcome. Several times I explained all of the problems associated with flying in northern latitudes, but each response was the same. Are you sure of your calculations. The reply of "I know I'm sure" didn't take long to turn into a "I think I'm sure" and finally to a "hope I'm sure." These doubts from his unrelenting questioning made my task even more demanding. Finally, a statement from one of my navigational instructors came to light when I distinctly remembered his most emphatic remark: "Never doubt your own ability. You and you alone in the airplane you might be flying in, knows how to do celestial navigation. All your training has to be applied and then utilized with confidence."

Within several minutes of the E.T.A. (estimate time of arrival) of landfall, we were informed by several crew members that Iceland was within sight. I sent a slight adjustment for a new heading to bring us over the airstrip at Reykjavik and the safety of good old mother earth. Cobb put the plane down but he did everything but grease it in. We bounced several times and squealed our brakes and landed like a ruptured duck. It was not a good landing. It seemed that the harder Frank tried, the poorer the results.

After a day's rest, we took off on the next leg to Nutts Corner, Ireland, a field located several miles from the city of Belfast. Once again we had a mediocre landing that only has significance in the complete picture of all the subsequent events regarding Cobb. It was not apparent to the crew at the time, but hind sight dictates that a pattern of misfortunes was developing. The crew members were excited and experiencing the thrill of seeing new and different countries and cultures. We were anxious and filled with expectations about our role as a bomber crew and the part we would play in the war.

Cobb, on the other hand, was evidently burdened with doubts and fears about the months that lay ahead. His mood was changing from one of cockiness and confidence to one of solemnness. I recall that Waddy and I decided to ignore a direct order restricting us to the base by slipping over the fence and avoiding guards to spend the night in Belfast. Cobb was invited but chose not to join us.

The following two days were spent in route to our new permanent base at Horham, England. Our new plane was taken away from us, and we were informed that we would be issued another one once we were reestablished. A boat trip and a lengthy train ride across southern England brought us to a small village located midway between Norwich and Ipswich, north of London. We were assigned to the 336th Squadron of the 95th Bombardment Group of the Eighth Air Force. The 95th was a unit of the 13th Wing along with the 100th and the 390th BG., all in the 3rd Division. The 95th was known as the Box B, a large black square was painted on each side of the tail with a large white B in the center. The 100th was the Box D and the 390th the Box J.

Several days after we settled in at Horham, one of our gunners informed us he spotted our original B-17 parked on one of the ramps at our base. There she was..... old No. 297334, in all her glory. We had Cobb check to see if we could reclaim this ship and were told that it would be assigned to our ten member team along with another ten member ground crew. It was mutually decided by the entire crew that the name of this B-17 would be "HAARD LUCK," a timely, stupid expression that was heard among flying personal every time a person made a statement seeking a little sympathy or encouragement. My job during the first several weeks of training was to paint a pretty little redheaded gal on each side of the nose of "our" plane, along with the chosen name. This little doll had an up-turned horseshoe in her red hair; two dangling dice for ear rings; in one up raised hand she held a left-handed monkey wrench and in the other was a four leaf clover; her brassiere consisted of two black eight balls; and her waist was covered just barely by a white bandana decorated with red hearts and diamonds along with black clubs and spades. Each of our leather A-2 jackets would also receive this very special lady.

When we had finished our training missions to orient us with bunchers, splashers, formation flying, firing our 50 cal. machine guns, different signal flares, etc., etc., we were now ready to pay a visit to Germany or parts of Europe held by the Germans and to start the first of the required 35 missions. As it turned out because of a shortage of navigators, I flew two missions with other crews before Cobb and the rest of the crew had a chance to start their tour of duty. The shortage of navigators and first pilots was due to the tactics of the German fighter pilots. They learned early that the most effective way to approach a B-17 formation was diving from the front and slightly from the right. This was referred to by the gunners as "eleven o'clock high." Because of this strategy, first pilots and navigators experienced the highest casualties.

My enthusiasm for war lasted through my first mission, which was a relatively close target that was located at Laon Athies near Paris. Only moderate amounts of flak and no German fighters appeared. However, my whole attitude changed on my second mission. Again, I had to fly with yet another crew. At early morning briefing, we all were amazed when the curtain was pulled back to expose a target deep in Europe, all the way to Czechoslovakia. The colored yarn bent its way around thumb tacks starting at Horham and broke several places across France and Germany until it reached the target at Brux, a synthetic oil refinery. The mission was over 1300 miles and we were hit by hundreds of FW190, ME109, and ME 110's both going and returning. At the target we were greeted by walls of intense flak. For nearly two hours I saw B-17's falling from the sky, both to the target and then on the return. At 1105 just south of Frankfurt, Lt. E.M. Yablonski's plane left the formation and exploded just after two chutes were spotted. All members of this 95th crew were killed except R.M Harbeck, the radio operator, and G.V. Dimazo, the ball turret gunner.

I mention these two missions because they gave me an experience my own crew had still to realize. I look back now and remember the different reactions I received from the "Haard Luck" crew as I related a blow-by-blow account of this harrowing mission. Cobb did not share my excitement nor really wanted to hear about it. The others had an opposite interest.

On my third mission, I was scheduled to fly with Lt. Cobb and the guys. They felt the same excitement that I had felt on my first mission. Constant chattering on the intercom was a way of covering up the obvious anxiety. Cobb repeatedly got mad and chewed the fellows out. He seemed to be especially on edge. On this day, May 13th, 1944, we flew to Osnabruck, Germany. The target was in the northern part of enemy territory, so some distance and time would be connected with the mission. Since this was Haard Luck's first trip with an inexperienced crew, she had to fly in a "tail-end charley" position . . . . low and in the back of the formation. We experienced some fighters and a modest amount of flak. All in all, as missions go, this one was mild; however, after we "had bombs away" we got a call from Cobb throwing out the idea that we ought to consider leaving the formation and sweating out the war in Sweden, a neutral country. We all took this remark as a joke and nothing further was said about it. This perhaps was a mistake.

Six days later the Cobb crew was scheduled to hit a marshalling yard on the east side of Berlin. Fighter activity was intense and the flak at the target was devastating. After bombs away, Lt. W.S. Waltman and his crew pulled away from the formation and stated that they had problems and were going to try and make it to Sweden. Cobb called down to me to give a compass heading to this neutral country as he started to swing the plane on a northern direction. I called to Waddy, co-pilot, and asked what was wrong. His reply was that there did not appear to be any real damage to the plane and that all instruments were functioning normally. I took Lt. Weakland's 45 cal. pistol and went up behind the two pilots. Lt. Cobb understood my concern. Waddy took over the controls and Cobb was informed that we would pull back into the formation and head for home. This incident should have been reported, but it wasn't. Another mistake.

The next day we were scheduled for an airfield near Brussels, Belgium. There was only a small amount of flak and no further problems with Cobb. He had isolated himself pretty much from the rest of the crew. On May 24th we were again listed for a possible mission to Berlin. We were a spare and would only make the trip if someone else had engine problems or for some other reason could not go on. No one aborted so at mid—Channel we were ordered to return to base. Weakland had already pulled the pins on forty 100# incendary bombs and it was his responsibility to replace each pin before landing. These pins keep the propeller from spinning and thus arming the bombs. The task was just completed as we got back to the base. We had 4000 pounds of bombs and nearly a full capacity of fuel.

Lt. Cobb came in hot, touched down late, was running out of runway, and he came down hard on the brakes. The right tire blew and the whole wheel assembly collapsed, causing the plane to groundloop and skid past the end of the runway. Because of the danger of blowing up or at least a bad fire, no one lost much time in putting as much distance between the hazard and safety. I looked back and saw that Cobb had made the mistake of trying to leave the cockpit via his side window and in the process had his leg and one boot stuck. I returned to help him just as he pulled his foot free and jumped to the ground. The plane did not blow, but it was severely damaged. Both props on the right side had their blades bent back, the wing tip had been torn up, and of course the wheel assembly crushed. Poor old "Haard Luck" would be out of action for some time. (Note: No.297334 did get back into action. On Sept. 11, 1944 Lt. Moore and his crew, flying our old plane, were knocked out of the sky and ended up being POW's for the duration of the war.)

I could really feel for Frank because I knew that he would have to justify the cause for the accident. The added weight of the bombs and the load of fuel would alter the attitude of the plane on landing and would require some adjustment for the approach and touchdown, but these were corrections that all pilots are taught. At the briefing Waddy, Weakland, and I decided that we had to tell of some of the previous incidents that should have been reported. These things, plus several notations on Lt Cobb's record, finally caught up with him. He was relieved of his status as first pilot. He flew later as co-pilot on another crew for several missions.

I look back on all of this with regret because I merely wrote Lt. Cobb off as being a coward and had very little to do with him. I feel especially bad about my juvenile reaction because I now know he needed friends—true and good friends. We could have and should have been with him through the fears and horrible moments that he must have been living. Each of us had to confront fear and the realization that war—and all of its consequences—was terrible and didn't make any sense, but we all seemed to be lucky because we could control these new and unreal emotions. Some guys threw up nearly every mission and some even relieved themselves in their flying suits. Waddy and I handled our pressures by excessive drinking and smoking. Each flyer had to resolve these horrible pressures in their own way. Frank seemed to keep it all inside.

Because I was not there to help a fellow crew member like I should have, I did not know all of the reasons nor outcome of Lt. Cobb's subsequent flights. I did find out, however, that he was reassigned as a tail gunner on lead planes in order to use his experiences as a pilot to observe and report on the quality of the formation. During my tour of duty, I became a lead navigator and subsequently flew with 19 different lead crews. Cobb never flew in any of the planes to which I was assigned.

Just a few months ago, I received a piece of information that helped to put all of these related parts into proper perspective. This information came 45 years late, but I sincerely believe that it is the key to why Lt. Cobb was not able to cope like the rest of the crew. One exception was Lt. Ray Weakland. Weakland, because of many personal problems, finally broke down and was sent home with an honorable discharge. The information about Cobb that came into my hands was a newspaper article written in a Crown Point, Indiana, newspaper back in 1944. A picture of our entire crew was sent to the paper by the public relation department on our base. The article that appeared with this picture identified each crew member and went on to tell about Lt. Cobb's father. Cobb's dad had been in World War I and had distinguished himself as a war hero. Besides the usual medals he received in war, his father also received the Distinguished Service Medal and for bravery in the Argonne Campaign he received the Croix de Guerre from the French.

I now believe that the image of his father and the footsteps Cobb tried to follow were beyond his capabilities. Instead of realizing that he was his own person with his own personality and inner strengths, Frank tried to walk in his dad's shoes. He was carrying a cross that was more than any one person could bear. Monday morning quarterbacking is always easy, but I shall always believe that each member of our crew could have been more supportive had we known all of the facts related to this true but sad story.

I have lost all track of Frank Cobb. On one of my trips through Crown Point, Indiana, I checked and could not find an address for him nor his parents. I would truly like to let him know how sorry I am for my actions.

Being classified as a hero or a coward are only words. I now know that neither one really exists. Heroes are people who are in the right place at the right time, with the right experiences, attitudes, and emotions. Cowards are people who are in the wrong place, at the wrong time, with experiences that do not prepare them for the exact moment. These two words no longer have any real meaning to me.

One final fact I learned from the newspaper article that made mention of the exploits of his father. Lt. Frank Cobb, during his high school days, was an Interscholastic Champion of the Pacific Coast in freestyle swimming. Few could claim that distinction Frank.

 B-17 Flying Fortress

Many have called this beautiful lady The Queen of the Sky. Because I have spent many hundreds of hours in her, traveled nearly 100,000 miles, and successfully completed 35 missions over Europe, I shall always have a special place for this B-17 in my memories. This airplane was conceived early enough, back in the early 1930s, so that when WWII broke out that it was possible to modify it and get it into production rather rapidly. It is the single most important reason the Allies were able to invade the continent and push the Germans back into their own country and ultimate defeat.

These results, however, were not cheap. From July 4, 1942, through May 1945, the Germans destroyed over 4,900 B-17s. This price was expensive, since each plane carried ten airmen. The havoc caused by this armada made victory possible. By June 6, 1944, the infamous D-DAY, General Dwight Eisenhower made the following observation in an address directed to the Eighth Air Force: "Because of the unrelenting bombing of targets throughout Europe by the Allied Bombers Command, the Germans are trying to move supplies they no longer have, with trains that have no engines, over tracks and bridges that do not exist, with trucks that will not move because they have no fuel, with machines that will not function because of the lack of ball bearings and with personnel that have become completely demoralized." All of this took time at a high, but necessary cost, and the B-17 played a huge role in this scenario. Just what kind of plane played such an important part during its period in history?

The following information will give a detailed account of what made this lady "tick" and how the men who flew her managed to do their jobs despite terrible odds. The plane, at the beginning of our entry into the war in mid-1942 was designated the B-17E. By July 17, 1943, the first raid with the modified B-17F took place. Neither of these two versions of the Flying Fortress had chin turret guns. During these early months of the American involvement in the war, the Eighth Bomber Command gained momentum as thousands of US airmen took great armadas of these planes over to Europe, which improved the bombing techniques that would eventually cripple the Nazi's war machine. However, the German fighter pilots probed and found the weak spot on these early B-17s; the plane proved vulnerable to head-on attacks.

Various hasty modifications were made to provide extra nose guns to cover this chink in the much publicized armour. Along with modified tail guns, with perfection in formation flying and additional experience, the B-17G was prepared to complete the job it was intended to do. It is also important to state that American fighter escort, made up of the P-47 Thunderbolt, the P-38 Lightening, and the famous P-51 Mustang, provided additional protection when they carried dropable wing fuel tanks that permitted them to escort all the way to distant German targets. These were our "little friends."

The B-17Gs, as with the previous models, were flown with a complete crew of ten, which was made up of four officers and six enlisted men. The B-17G was classified as an all-metal land plane, low-wing cantilever monoplane, long-range, high-altitude bomber built by the Boeing Air-craft Co. of Seattle, Washington. The Statistics for the B-17G are given in Table 1.

The crew was dispersed throughout this plane, with the four officers in the front protion, while the six gunners were positioned along the length of the fuselage. The bombardier was seated in the nose with a large plexiglass bubble to give him the best possible observation point in the plane. He sat behind a Norden Bomb Sight with a switch to open the bomb bay doors and another toggle switch to release individual bombs or the entire load. He could also control the action of the aircraft by using his bomb sight when the plane was on automatic pilot. Below the bombardier were twin .50 cal. machine guns mounted in an electrically-powered Bendix Chin Turret. Prior to the installation of this chin turret, the casualty loss for first pilots and navagators was excessive because of the German fighter strategy of mounting frontal attacks. It is important to note that most bombardiers did not use their Norden Bomb Sights, but rather opened the bomb doors when the lead ship did so and then dropped their bombs when the Lead Bombardier signalled "bombs away." Only the best bombardiers were given the responsibility of flying in the lead plane.

Right behind the bombardier, the navigator had a small desk mounted on the left side of the nose. On the left of this desk was mounted a British Gee radar instrument that utilized a cathode ray tube to display information. It had limited value because the Germans constantly jammed it over Europe. Above the navigator was an astro dome of plexiglas for celestial navigation. Shots would be taken of the sun and stars using a sextant. In front of the navigator, there were flight instruments such as a compass, altimeter, oxygen gage, and thermometer. On the floor under the table was a navigational case containing star books and a variety of small instruments. The flight map with the predetermined mission laid out was always on the desk, and it was on this map that the navigator kept his notes and all calculations. The main instrument that was used constantly was an E6B computer, from which ground speed; air speed; direction; fuel consumption; fuel remaining in tanks; points of no-return; ETA to target or base; (and whatever information might prove helpful or necessary to the pilots) was computed. The navigator took the responsibility of keeping notes of planes sighted, fighters shot down, bombers leaving formation, number of parachutes spotted from falling bombers, potential enemy targets, bomb results, and any other important data.

TABLE 1

```
Wing:
      Span    103 ft. 10 inches
      Area    1420 sq. ft.
Fuselage:     74 ft. 4 in
Tail unit:
      fin area—143 sq. ft.
      rudder area—39 sq. ft.
      tail plane area—331 sq. ft.
Height:   19 ft. 1 in
Landing Gear:  electrical retraction
Main wheels—55" dia.
Tail wheels—26" dia.
Power Plant:   4 Wright Cyclone R-1820, nine cylinder air cooled radial with
      exhaust-driven turbo-super chargers.  1000 hp each
Fuel:   2810 US Gallons
Bomb Load:   4000 lbs (up to 13,600# w/ external racks)
Propellers:   11 ft.7 in. dia., three-blade feathering, constant speed
Weight:   36,135# empty, 55,000# normal load, 72,000# maximum load
Speed:   287 mph at 25,000 ft.; 182 mph cruise speed; 90 mph landing speed
Service ceiling:   35, 600 ft.
Range:   2000 miles
No. Built:
      B-17E.....512
      B-17F....3405
      B-17G....8680
Bombs:   4000# (normal internal load-long range)
         17,600# (6 × 1600# internal plus 2 × 4000#ext.)
Guns:   13 .50 calibre Browning M-2 machine guns
```

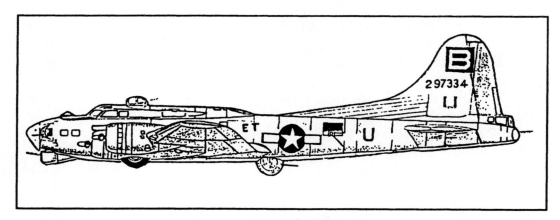

B-17 Flying Fortress

This information was given to the Interrogation Officer at the completion of each mission. The above tasks were performed primarily by lead navigators and those who were conscientious. Many navigators in planes behind the lead ship would just keep track of their position so that in an emergency they could give their pilot directions to return to their base or some neutral country, such as Switzerland or Sweden.

Late in 1944, on missions where weather obscured the target area, a PFF navigator was sometimes sent in special planes equipped with radar. Using Pathfinder Radar Equipment, he would more accurately locate the target through dense cloud cover. The navigator compartment had two .50 cal. machine guns mounted in "cheak" mountings, staggered on each side of the nose. These guns were less than useless because of the limited swing action and sight restrictions. Once I became a lead navigator (after my ninth mission), I completely forgot that I had these guns because of all the other responsibilities.

Next to and slightly above the navigator there were two seats where the first pilot sat on the left and the co-pilot sat on the right. All controls to fly this lady were at the fingertips of each of the pilots. The plane responded well and many unbelievable stories were recorded of severely damaged planes making it back to safety because of the durability of construction and the skill of the men who flew it. Tight formation flying was the most demanding, especially in turbulent air and at altitudes where contrails were present.

On bomb runs from the I.P.(Initial Point) to the target, each plane had to fly straight and level, regardless of flak. At other times slight evasive action could be taken, like momentarily lifting a wing to avoid some flak. Perhaps the pilots' most difficult task was to fly in formation through flak and enemy fighter attacks without having a gun to expend emotions or vent anger.

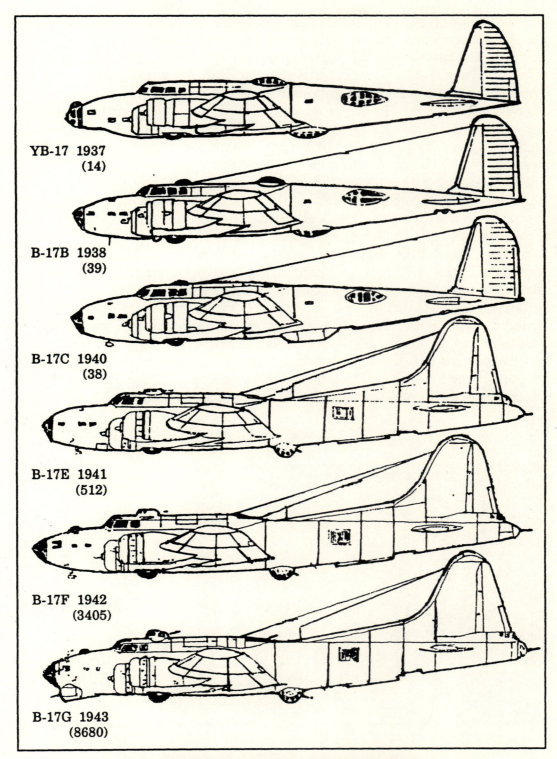

The Evolution of the B-17 Flying Fortress
(Note: I flew in the B-17F & B17G)

The top turret gunner was located right behind the pilots. His twin .50 cal. guns were mounted in an electrically-powered Sperry Turret. He sat on a seat that gave him 360° turning capability and the ability to observe all enemy action that occurred in the top half of an imaginary sphere. The sargeant manning this important gun placement was also the engineer on each plane. He was mechanically inclined and perhaps the best trained of all of the gunners. He was called upon to fix minor problems during flight, but most important, to report to the ground crews between flights. He truly was a key man on the crew.

The next compartment on the plane did not house any personnel, but it did hold the bombs until they could be dropped. Above the bomb bay doors there was a narrow cat walk or ramp as a passage to connect the front and rear of the plane. Flexibility was designed in the bomb racks and shackles so that they could handle anything from 100# incendiary bombs to larger 1600# general demolition bombs. The bombs themselves varied drastically from anti-personnel, delayed action, incendiary, deep penetration, demolition, and so forth. The type we carried was determined by Operations, depending on the specific target, and were loaded during the night before a mission by armament crews. The usual bombs had propellers mounted in the nose that would unscrew as the bomb dropped, thus arming it. The safety device was a small pin that had to be removed once the plane was airborne and before bombs away. This was

B-17 Gunnery Positions

Radio compartment looking forward. Bomb bay is on other side of bulkhead.

Above photograph by USAF

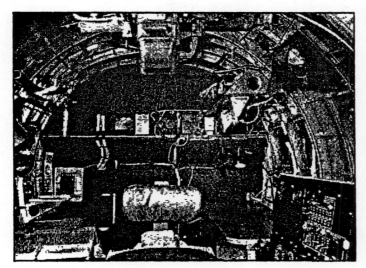

Interior view of navigator's work area.

Waist-gun positions. With open windows, temperatures dropped to 40° below zero.

Above photographs by USAF

Radio operator's gun position.

the responsibility of the bombardier. In the bomb bay, there was also a funnel to the outside of the plane in which a crew member could urinate if it proved necessary. There was no toilet on board. Using this funnel at altitude (i.e., at 50 degrees below zero) with a portable oxygen bottle in a bouncing plane was a major undertaking. One can only imagine the problems associated with not being able to control other body functions.

B-17 Gunnery Positions

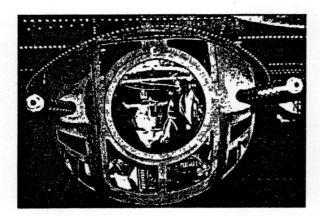

Ball-turret gunner.

Tail-gun positon.

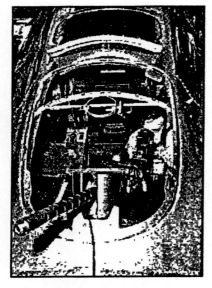

Top-turret gunner.

Radio operator's gun position.

Photographs by USAF

The next compartment was for the radio operator. His radio equipment was on the front wall of this compartment, with a small desk and seat below. With his equipment he could monitor his home base, other planes, and sometimes enemy installations. He could assist the navigator by getting updated weather information. In the B-17F, the radio operator had a single .50 cal. machine gun that was mounted at the ceiling of his compartment. It was about as useful as the machine guns of the navigator. The G Model 17 eliminated this gun for obvious reasons.

The ball turret gunner had his position located at the mid-section of the plane and protruding below the fuselage. The ventral position had a Sperry electrically-powered turret shaped like a ball with twin .50 cal. machine guns. The quarters were cramped and the ball was extremely cold up at altitude (usually above 25,000 ft.) with temperatures in the minus 50 to 60 degree range. This gunner was usually the smallest member of the crew and could operate this interesting turret in any position, which covered the lower half of a sphere. This, in turn, complimented the top turret gunner.

The two waist gunners were in the center of the plane. Their positions were slightly staggered and each gunner had a hand-held, belt-fed .50 cal M-2 that was fired through an open window. Their position was extremely noisy and very cold. Many waist gunners lost fingers because of frost bite when they had to repair jammed guns. These gunners fired their guns from a standing position; and during the heat of battle, they had to be very careful not to fire at other planes in the formation or to hit the wing of their own aircraft.

Last, but certainly not least, there was our tail gunner. He was cramped into a tight compartment at the remote tail position. He fired twin hand-operated Brownings with a remote ring and bead-sight. His job was to protect the rear of the formation. He, like the ball turret gunner, had a difficult job just getting in and out of his position. It sometimes made a big difference when the plane had to be abandoned prior to an explosion or a tight spin. Each crew member had to wear bulky warm clothing, had to move about with head sets and their connecting wires, had to have a throat mike wire attached to the plane, had to wear an oxygen mask above 10,000 ft., and sometimes had to be hooked up with a wire for a heated flight suit. You had to be careful that you did not turn completely around or otherwise all or some of these life support umbilical cords would be pulled away. Without the head-set and throat-mike connected, you would be without sound or voice contact. If this happened and the oxygen were also disconnected, you could die in a few minutes without realizing that you even had a problem. During enemy action, the floor at all positions would be littered with spent hot .50 cal. cartridges. When the guns were fired, the entire plane would vibrate. The noise of these guns, the roar of the four 1000 horsepower engines, and the nervous shouts over the intercom from the different gun positions calling out the direction of German plane attacks was unreal. These were moments that made men sweat despite the negative temperature.

This plane was truly The Queen Of The Sky. The B-17s in the 95th Bomb Group flew a total of 321 missions with a total credited sorties of 8903. This Group dropped 19,770 tons of bombs on targets in all parts of occupied Europe. A total of 157 planes were shot down with another 39 lost from other operations. The Group had the highest German fighter plane kill in the Eighth Air Force with 425 destroyed, 117 probably destroyed, and 231 damaged.

As important a role as the B-17 played in the total effort, the men who flew her were equally up to the task. Roger Freeman, A Britisher and one of the leading authorities on U.S. Warplanes, states:

The Eighth Air Force was not without its share of human failures, tactical blunders and mistaken policies. These short-comings were, nevertheless, far outweighed by the development, to a unique degree, of such admirable characteristics as a remarkable esprit de corps, dogged bravery and supreme determination to succeed. It was, indeed, these attributes which have so rightly conferred upon the Eighth the honor of becoming one of the most famous military organizations in history.

Box B to Big B

For the past week, the weather had been lousy. Today, Wednesday, May 18, 1944, was no exception. The rain, poor visibility, and mountainous cloud banks extended all the way into Europe. The 95th Bomb Group had not flown a mission since May 13th, when we hit Osnabruck, Germany.

Our primary target on that day was a marshalling yard, and it turned out to be a particularly rough mission, both because of German fighter planes and the amount of flak over the city. This mission to northern Germany had been my third experience in combat, but it was the very first for my original crew. Each of us knew we were expected to fly 25 missions (later extended to a total of 30 by General Curtis LeMay and soon after, to a grand total of 35 missions by General "Jimmy" Doolittle) so we were "gnashing at the bit" to get on with it. We never knew, until late in the evening, whether there would be a mission the next day or not. At the same time, we would also learn whether we would be scheduled to take part in this mission. The primary concern of the Eighth Air Force Command was the weather over the Continent and specifically over the target. These were decisions in which we had no input so we soon learned to take each day as it came.

Late in the afternoon on this gloomy Wednesday, I was involved in one of our usual poker games with five other friends in our barracks. We were sitting on our cots concentrating on the game of seven card draw, when someone came in and announced that they had just put up a fair weather alert flag at squadron headquarters. This only implied that the forecast for better weather was predicted for tomorrow and that it would be likely that the 95th would get to fly Group Sorty Number 131. It was apparent that somebody knew something that we didn't. The weather conditions at the moment were so cold and damp that we all had on our A-2 flight jackets in the barracks. It was cold for a day in May, but rather typical for England. Perhaps there is a sun out there somewhere.

Deciding to forego supper, Dan Waddell, Weakland, and I strolled over to the Officers Club. We knew two important things at this moment. First, a few bottles of hard to get bourbon would be opened at 1700 hours.

54 • Box B to Big B

Officer's Club

Mess Hall

Briefing Room at Operations

Colonel Dave McKnight

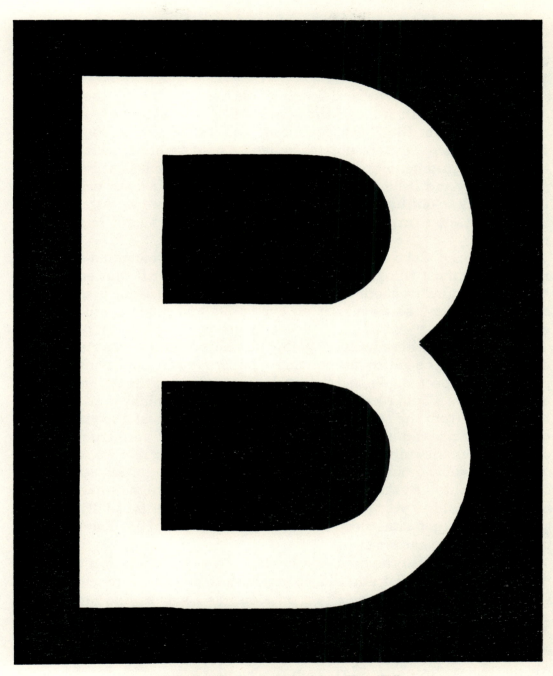

95th Bomb Group Marking-Box "B"
(Symbol placed on tail and wing surface of B-17)

And second, that the bar would close down at 2000 hours if, in fact, there was a mission tomorrow. We guessed right. Just as we ordered a last drink, the operation officer posted the crews scheduled to fly on GSN #131.

Weakland walked over and finally made his way through the anxious officers gathered in front of the board. "Yep, there it was." C-ll, Lt. Cobb's crew from the 336th Squadron, would take part in the mission tomorrow. Also we were not scheduled as a spare crew, which meant that if all equipment worked, we would make the mission. Weakland gave Waddy and I the news and the three of us finished our drinks and headed back to our barracks. We didn't know where we were going, but the important thing was that we were scheduled to get in another mission.

We informed Cobb about the "good news" and his reception made us realize that most things are relative. Cobb was not all that enthused, and he reminded us of our last mission to Osnabruck. None of us appreciated a "kill-joy" so we all sat on our bunks and made small talk for another hour.

We wondered where we were going; just how good the weather would be; or whether the entire mission might be scrapped if conditions did not improve as expected. We had the usual concerns about the type of fighter escort that we would receive and whether they could make it all the way to and back from the selected target. It had been almost a month to the day that we arrived at Horham from the States. We were trucked into the base from the railroad station on April 17th and tonight was the 18th of May. A whole month had gone by and we were just getting started on our tour of duty. At the rate we were going, it would take us over a year before we could expect to be sent home. Finally, we mutually agreed that we had to get some sleep because we knew that an 0300 hour wake-up call was not that far away.

Once you get into the sack and lay back, you enter a world of silent thoughts. Now the war and the job you have to do turns into a very personal one. Each night prior to a mission, as I was to find out in the ensuing months, I would spend an hour or more mulling over my thoughts, doubts, and even hopes. This period was a waste of time because you were unable to come up with answers. You ultimately realized that the "fickle finger of fate" would rule supreme and would be the deciding factor in how events turned out.

After a tasteless breakfast that had been overpowered by too many cigarettes, we signed in at the Briefing Room at Operations and settled down in this noisy, smokey space. It was here that we would learn what and where the target would be; the route we would take; the information on flak areas to avoid, if possible; the fighter escort rendezvous points, and times; slide shots of the actual target and the area around it; and any other information that would prove helpful to the success of the mission.

Colonel Carl Truesdell entered the noisy room; everyone popped to attention and you could immediately hear a pin drop. The colonel put us at ease and directed that the curtain concealing our target be pulled back. Before he could speak, we could see that this trip would take us deep into Germany and that a great portion of our flight would be over the North Sea.

The colonel removed his customary cigar and told us that the target would be Berlin, that we would cross over near Denmark, north of Hamburg, and that we would approach the target from the northwest, giving us a fair sized tail wind for the bomb run. We were told that this was to be a maximum effort by the Eighth Air Force and that all three Divisions would be hitting targets in and around Berlin. The captive audience of about 400 men was informed that Colonel Dave McKnight would lead the 95th today and that our specific target for the entire 13th Wing would be the rail center near the center of the city. Several railroad lines converged at this point with many buildings included within the drop zone.

After the general briefing, all navigators were required to attend an additional briefing to obtain specifics on our route to the target, our I. P. Point, details of landmarks immediately around the target area, rally point, weather, fighter escort coverage and where and when we could expect to see them, and some suggested things to observe while over Europe in order to report to intelligence.

When I finally got out to the hardstand where "HAARD LUCK" was parked, I could see the other members of the crew mulling around. This is an anxious period for everyone, this waiting to get going. Once you get underway, each member of the crew has specific duties to perform and this is the very thing that each is geared to do at this early hour of the morning. The gunners are joking and pushing each other around, trying to conceal their inner thoughts. Cobb and Waddy, our pilot and co-pilot, want to pick up any additional data that I may have from my briefing. Weakland, our bombardier, wants the weather report at the target area and what type of fighter escort we could expect. Our six gunners, Eavenson, Newswanger, Argyrakis, Tomchek, Fleet, and Ellender, were really charged up.

Others that were equally interested and concerned were the ten members of our ground crew. They had been working all night repairing any plane damage from a previous mission, checking instruments, tuning up the four large engines, loading up ammo at each of the thirteen machine guns, filling the bomb bay with the types of bombs we were to carry, filling the fuel tanks so that they are full, and doing anything else that's required to make our work more efficient. I can't say enough for their dedication. Their work place was mostly outside in the heat, cold, wind, rain or whatever.

"HAARD LUCK", no. 297334, was the same plane our crew had flown over the Atlantic from Grand Island, Nebraska. We all loved this plane and each believed she would carry us through the war unscathed. This was not to be the case, but on this morning of May 19th, we believed it to be true.

Lt. Cobb and Lt. Waddell started the first engine at 0736 hours, followed by the other three. The stationary aircraft began to vibrate and come to life. The adrenalin started flowing as the roar of the engines from 39 bombers woke up the English countryside. Slowly, ever so slowly, this 65,000 pound monster moved out of the hardstand and onto the perimeter. We pulled in behind Lt. Sheehan and his crew in no. 231410. There were about twenty B-17s moving slowly down each perimeter paved path, one behind the other. The only noise one could hear above those of the engines was the squeak of the brakes. Just about the time that these two long columns stopped, two green flares exploded skyward and our leader began to roll down the 7,000 foot runway into what little wind existed.

One after another, these planes took off at 30 second intervals. The first real apprehension comes with take off. As we gradually pick up airspeed moving down this mile and one-quarter bumpy ribbon of concrete, the constant hope is that we will reach the critical speed to lift this clumsy beast into the air. Part way down this runway is the point of no return, when it is no longer possible to stop the plane and all available power is needed to lift the 32 tons of metal, gasoline, bombs, and crew over obstacles that are racing toward you. In the event that the plane cannot get airborne, then the 2,800 gallons of gas and the eight 500 pound bombs will have their day in one glorious moment as the plane crashes into a VHF tower at the end of the runway. With a slight bounce on the heavy rubber tires, Cobb pulls back on the controls and we stutter into the thin air.

Once this cumbersome load is lifted into the air, this same craft is transformed into a graceful and beautiful Flying Fortress. It is perhaps the best designed plane of all time. Its function and durability met all of the criteria at the right time in the right war. Much was asked of her, much was expected from her, and much was received from her.

Our next concern was the 6,000 feet of clouds that we had to climb through in order to reach our designated altitude. Each B-17, on a predesignated course, would fly blind thru this soup. It would be impossible to see our wings and complete dependence was on flying by instruments alone. One by one, the big birds with the large block B popped out of the top of this cloud cover and had visibility once again. Many hundreds of aircraft and crews were lost during the war due to collisions of two or more planes in these ever present cloud covers. This was a risk that had to be taken, however. All planes headed toward Buncher 8 near Great Yarmouth on the coast of East Anglia. As we climbed to reach altitude, each plane gradually pulled into their assigned position in the formation. Shortly after we headed out over the North Sea, all four Squadrons of the 95th B.G. were in position in the formation.

We climbed to 27,000 ft. altitude on a course of approximately 78°. Two of our planes, "Slightly Dangerous" with Lt. Herchenhahan's crew and "Torando" with Lt. Greenwald's crew, never could find our formation and were left behind. Spares filled in their slot while additional spares, namely Lt. Lempert in 231924, and Lt. McCall in 231939 and plane no. 23400, all returned to Base. We were now 32 strong, flying in a tight formation with the B-17s from the 334th, 335th, 336th, and the 412th Squadrons making up the famous 95th Bomb Group.

This was the 10th visit to Berlin by the 95th, but it was the first mission to the German capital that gave the notoriety to our Bomber Group. On March 4, 1944, the Eighth Air Force had sent out several hundred planes to hit Berlin for the first time. As they approached the target area, the word went out to abort the mission. All groups returned or hit alternate targets, except the 95th. The 95th believed this message was transmitted by the Germans and consequently ignored the recall and were alone over the target. Our Group was presented with a Presidential Unit Citation for this action. Four B-17s were lost and another nine were badly damaged but the 95th was "first over Berlin."

Today the 95th, along with the 100th, and the 390th Bomb Groups, making up the 13th Combat Wing, headed once again toward Germany's most sacred target. Our Wing, plus the 45th and 4th Wings, made up the complete 1st Division. We would hit various targets within the city of Berlin, while the planes of the 2nd and 3rd Divisions would find targets in cities in the immediate area. If all squadrons had the strength of the 95th, then our Division would bring approximately 300 planes to the target. Today's endeavor by the 8th would send close to 1,000 bombers to Der Vaterland. It would only be a month till this number doubled.

After we reached an altitude of 27,000 feet, the order was given to test fire our 50 caliber machine guns. Each plane took on new vibrations as a dozen guns were fired in short bursts. My job as navigator was just beginning. We left England and were heading in a northeast direction toward the Denmark-German border. Our plane position in the formation was as a "tail-end Charlie" in the low Squadron. I later learned that this

Bomb door open—Bombs away—A taste of flak

Target—Sythetic fuel and chemicals

was one of the hairiest places in the formation, both from flak and from German fighter attacks. I guess everybody has got to be some place.

As a relatively new navigator, my primary duty was to keep track of our progress and position at all times so that, should we be required to leave the protection of the formation, I could direct the pilot on a safe course back to our base at Horham. In order to perform these required functions, I believe one should realize some additional limitations in which we had to work. A crew member of a B-17 flying at 27,000 feet was subjected to temperatures of minus 50 F., with a noise level that was almost deafening, caused by the four 1200 horsepower engines, and a constant vibration and buffeting at this five mile altitude. This same crew member had to perform in a heavy clumsy flying suit, gloves and fur boots, all heated electrically. He wore a helmet with built-in headsets, covered his eyes with goggles and the rest of his face with an oxygen mask containing a microphone. Wires and hoses connected him to the airplane. Others in the plane wore a chest type parachute, plus a flak jacket that weighed another 15 pounds. The final distraction took place when you were attacked by fighters or when you reached the target area and were exposed to flak. It was most difficult to concentrate and to perform assigned tasks.

When one looks back and realizes that the pilots behind the controls may have been a construction worker or a farm boy from Kansas, the navigator a freshman engineering student, the bombardier a truck driver, and the gunners a grocery clerk or a service station attendant (or you name it), these unskilled kids who were quickly trained to fly and to handle this complex airplane, the B-17 did a great job.

We left the coast of England at 0828 hours and by 1100 hours we saw our first sign of flak off our right wing, which was a safe distance away. We were above a solid blanket of clouds but as a navigator, I knew that we were abreast of the Island of Helgoland. The Germans occupied this strategic piece of rock and never disappointed us by giving a continuous burst of flak. These black puffs of smoke in the shape of inverted "Y's" told us that we were on course and on time. Also, we now knew that the Germans would know that we were on our way. The important thing that they did not know was just which one of their cities would be today's target.

It might be worth noting an article in which the Berlin commander of anti-aircraft defenses told his people why it was impossible to prevent American daylight raids. Explaining why bombs sometimes dropped even before the Nazi "Actung Warning System" had begun to function, the Commander said that the alarms could not keep pace with the speed of the U.S. raiders. "There can be no doubt about the fact that it is absolutely impossible for us to prevent an air attack," he said. "We cannot do it."

We made landfall near the Danish-German border and altered course in a southeasterly direction, which took the formation just north of Kiel, Germany. It was here that the first fighters hit us. Several dozen FW-190s and ME 110s made a single pass at the 95th. Most of their effort, however, seemed to be directed at the 100th and the 390th Bomb Groups. Our gunners spotted seven B-17s going down.

At 1336 hours we reached our I. P. Point just northwest of Berlin, about seven miles from our designated target. The sky below us had large patches of clouds, probably 70 percent of the land below was obscured. At this same moment, all hell broke loose. The intensity of the flak was awesome. We were on our bomb run and all bomb bay doors were now open. We seemed to be just creeping through the threatening sky. Minutes seemed like an eternity. We had several hits from flak fragments, when suddenly we got a jolt that seemed to momentarily stop the plane. I looked backward just in time to see Sgt. Eavenson slump out of his harness from the top turret. He fell to the floor of the plane and was unconscious. He was only about six feet from me, so I was at his side within seconds. I could not find any blood or obvious wounds, but I did see a huge hole through his flight jacket collar and the top of his may-west was torn away. I got a portable oxygen bottle hooked up to his mask and he responded immediately. The back of his neck was badly bruised with a large protruding lump. The flak fragment had not entered his body. Jim rolled his eyes briefly and insisted on getting back to his position. There was no time to argue. A large piece of flak had cut through a strut on his turret, and its energy was mostly spent when it hit Eavenson.

All planes keyed on the lead ship and when they saw bombs away, each plane hit the switch and dumped their load. At the critical point in our bomb run, the target was completely covered by clouds. The order was given to close bomb bay doors and the entire Group made a 360° turn in order to make a second approach on our target. This was in lieu of going to a selected alternate target miles away on our return trip to England. Colonel McKnight felt that the clouds were breaking up and that they would be favorable within minutes. This meant another six or seven minutes over the target area. Again, we opened bomb bay doors and at the precise moment our 4,000 pounds of bombs were dropped in an impressive pattern. All this time the sky was black with flak patterns in all directions.

As we turned to get the hell away, we were suddenly hit from below. I could see the flash at the same time I heard it hit. My right leg was pulled or knocked from beneath me; and as I fell to the floor, I figured my number was up. I looked down and could see my lower body was covered with hundreds of large wood splinters. It looked terrible. I noticed that my right boot was torn apart with large pieces of wool protruding. I was afraid to look. The shell had hit the plane from below, slightly behind the chin turret, and numerous pieces had passed through the plywood floor in the navigator's area. This is the only wood in the entire aircraft. A large piece hit my boot but was mostly spent.

It didn't take too long to ascertain that I and the plane were in one piece. I could now look out and see additional flak bursts around us. We

Come Fly With Me • 63

were now leaving the perimeter of Berlin and the flak suddenly stopped. Our course would take us back to our original rally point and would put us on a course that should avoid additional flak. One of our planes was badly hit and slipped away from the formation; plane number 297290, "Smiling Sandy Sanchez" was piloted by Lt. Waltman. He radioed in that he could not hold his altitude with several engines out and that he would try and make it to Sweden. The other members of the crew were Lt. McCallon, co-pilot; Lt. Robertson, Navigator; Lt. Fournier, Bombardier; Sgt. Gossman, Engineer; Sgt. Myers, Radio Operator; Sgt. Brainard, Ball Turret Gunner; Sgt. Faust, Tail Gunner; and Sgts. Corpage & Wright, Waist Gunners. They were all interned at Akesholm, Sweden, for the duration of the war.

At the same time that Lt. Waltman was compelled to slide away from the formation, Lt. Cobb and our "Haard Luck" began to follow suit. This incident is described in more detail in another story and will not be dealt with here. Suffice it to state that our plane had received a great deal of battle damage but was capable of making it back to our Base. Lt. Waddell returned "Haard Luck" to the rear of the formation after taking the controls away from the first pilot.

Once we left the Continent and headed out over the North Sea, we felt that we could relax somewhat and perhaps assess some of the damage. We had many of our fighter escort present now and the danger of any further German fighter attacks was reduced. As I took off my oxygen mask to light up a cigarette, I noticed that my oxygen line behind me had been hit by flak, was bent away from the wall of the plane, and was pointing toward me. The line had been cut but still held the piece of flak. It was obvious that a little 0.25" ss steel tube had kept me from taking this fragment.

Next, I noticed that my navigational brief case and my work table had several flak fragments imbedded in them. I added these fragments, plus the one I retrieved from my boot, to a collection that I didn't care to enlarge on. About this time I had the realization that I was bleeding profusely from somewhere on my back. I could feel the blood running down my spine, even though there did not appear to be any pain connected with this sensation. I stepped over to Lt. Weakland and asked him to check. He slid his arm down the inside of my flight suit and retrieved it with a dirty laugh—it was sweat. Despite the sub-zero temperature, I had been sweating bullets. I knew that I had anxious moments and extreme concern, but I was unaware of my sweat glands working overtime. Later we found a large chunk of flak, about the size of my fist, below Jim Eavenson's turret. It had sheared off a main strut on the protruding turret, had tore up Jim's lifejacket, and had cut up the collar of his flight suite before hitting him in the back side of his neck. If this fragment had not been spent, it would have torn Jim's head off. Others in our plane had similar experiences.

The many moments we spent over Berlin were frightening and provided experiences that we could have lived without. Yet, each of us, in our own way, had to appreciate the fact that we were the lucky ones. There is no way to completely describe this experience with words. These are moments that had to be lived and suffered through, in order to give real meaning to the true definition of the word "experience." The sounds, the sights, the smells, and the helplessness one underwent can not be duplicated. The fear of death was not paramount, but the fear of what was to come next and how long would this intensity of emotions continue made time seem to stand still.

It was 1752 hours when we passed over the coast of East Anglia and we knew that we were only minutes away from Horham, our base. On the radio we could hear all of the pilots contacting the control tower that they had wounded aboard. These planes and the severely damaged aircraft would be given priority to land first. As they approached the runway, two flares were fired from planes with wounded aboard, thus alerting the medics and ambulances.

"Haard Luck" was one of the last planes to land. Today, this was considered a privilege, since we did not have wounded or dead comrades aboard. As we looked down on the field, we could see large groups of ground personnel and our fellow flyers gathered and waiting. The word had gotten out that this had been a rough mission. It turned out that the 95th was perhaps the luckiest, with 31 of the original 32 returning. Some Groups had many of their planes missing, planes that would not return.

The cost of this mission, or any other mission, cannot be measured in normal or usual terms. Perhaps it can only be judged by what it accomplished over the long haul, with this single endeavor considered with other such undertakings. When all of this has to be balanced with the extent of death and destruction rendered, perhaps only time will tell. Time does not often divulge this type of information.

After we landed and gingerly moved our B-17 back to its hardstand, we had a chance to relive, for a moment, this mission because each of the ground crew was more than interested. As we tried to assess all the damage, it was obvious that this day was not meant to be our last. One of the mechanics started counting holes in the plane and gave up after he had reached over 150. It was hard to believe that none of the ten crew members had been wounded. The # 2 engine had a feathered prop because an oil line had been cut, the top turret had to be replaced, and numerous holes patched. This would be done by morning. None of us knew at this moment that we had been scheduled to fly GSN#132; this time, the destination was Brussels, Belgium.

Forty-six years later, as I record this experience, I realize that I was truly fortunate to fly 35 missions over Europe. Some of these flights would be considered "milk-runs" and others would prove to be even rougher than this first trip to Berlin. I would return to Germany's capitol several more times before I finally completed my tour of duty. I have since learned that fate still follows each individual through life. At the age of 69, I have lost many of my friends during the last 40 years. The demise of these friends had nothing to do with war, and each came as a disappointing surprise to me. Today, as in the war, I have resolved that each of us has our own moment or time. There is nothing we can do to alter this schedule, for myself or for others. I have always been grateful that our lives touched, but I know that each of us has to move on by making the most out of the moments that we have left. I guess time does divulge some things. It tells each of us to cherish it and to use it wisely.

 "Know Thy Enemy"

When I volunteered and entered the Army Air Force training program, I knew why I had made this important decision, and I also knew just what my country had to do. Being a college student at the time, I read and listened to all of the news pertaining to the German aggression throughout Europe. I followed on maps the surrender of each country to the German Wehrmacht. The Battle of Britain captured all of my sympathies for the people of England. The final push that I—and most other Americans—needed was provided by the Japanese and their dastardly attack on Pearl Harbor.

On December 7, 1941, I went to the Armory with my newfound friend, Norma Schmidt, to get the latest news about the attack on Hawaii. I was a member of the University of Wisconsin R.O.T.C. and was most interested in the news of this act. It was here that we learned of the death of two of my neighborhood friends from Wausau. Both were killed at Pearl Harbor on the Island of Oahu. Kermit Lavick was killed immediately on the runway at Wheeler Air Force Base and Don Plant was subsequently machine gunned down as he tried to pull his friend to safety. This brought the war home in an instant.

Throughout my training as a cadet in the U.S. Air Force, I did not think about the enemy, Germany or Japan, but instead concentrated wholeheartedly on the skills that I had to learn. Ultimately, I would be commissioned as a Lieutenant in the Air Force and be sent to England as a navigator. For the first time, I knew which of the two enemies that I would be confronting. Since I was the offspring of an Irish mother and a German father, I now entered the heart of this war with mixed emotions. On the way to combat with the crew I had been assigned to, we landed at Nutts Corner, Ireland. The very next night when I had arrived at my Base at Horham, England, we were bombed by a German plane, the first of only two such attacks. So much for my heritage.

The first time I was in close approximation with this unknown enemy was on my second mission. This particular raid was to a synthetic oil refinery in Brux, Czechoslovakia, over 600 miles from my sanctuary in

England. This mission was deep in the enemy territory and was all too typical of the techniques the Luftwaffe used to eliminate the planes of the Allies from German skies. They relied on fighter planes and flak.

When the Americans arrived in England, they decided to carry the war to Germany by means of daylight bombing missions. There was a great deal of controversy concerning this technique, since the British learned the hard way that to survive combat missions deep into the Fatherland they had to be conducted at night. Their daylight excursions resulted in intolerable losses of men and planes. The Americans learned this same lesson through the first year of operations. The 8th Air Force, General Eisenhower, and finally Prime Minister Winston Churchill agreed that the Americans would be permitted to continue this dangerous method of attack. Progress was constantly being made to improve the odds of survival for our crews. The huge sacrifice being made by those early crews was necessary to make the enemy pay and to hamper and impede their ability to continue the war.

The early formations of Flying Fortresses used B-17Es and B-17Fs. The German fighter pilot soon learned where these bold formations had weaknesses and logically developed methods that gave them some advantages for survival during an attack. The Germans learned that frontal attacks were the safest approach to the large formations of bombers. They knew that each plane had 10 or 11, 50 caliber machine guns and that the entire formation could expend a great deal of fire-power on a single target, especially if they could track it and had sufficient time. In reality, this was most difficult. The Germans knew that frontal attacks meant that the rate of closure was over 600 mph and that the formation had the least number of guns covering this direction.

The German fighter pilot would attack a formation of bombers by positioning their plane at a higher altitude, usually with the sun at their back. They would then dive into the group of bombers with the added speed of a power dive. The advantage of using the sun and even large cloud banks was that they could be well into their approach before being seen.

The only guns that could meet these frontal attacks from above were those of the top turret gunners. They had twin 50 cal. guns mounted in an electrically-powered Sperry Turret. These guns could swing in a 360° arc and could cover the upper half of a sphere. The complement to the top turret was the ball turret position. This gunner had the responsibility of a frontal attack from below. In a cramped ball with limited visibility, he also had to worry about the enemy approaching from all directions. The losses on these early raids into Germany were devastating. On some missions 40 or 60 planes would be shot down, each with 10 crewmen. It wasn't until early in 1944 that the B-17G began arriving in

England in large numbers. This Flying Fortress now was equipped with an electrically-powered Bendix Chin-turret with twin 50 cal. machine guns. These movable guns in the nose of each plane made a frontal attack as costly as from any other direction. German fighter pilots were constantly probing for weak points from which to attack. A copy of a German poster designed to instruct Luftwaffe pilots how to attack the B-17, a Viermotoriges Kampfflugzeug ("four engine fighter airplane") follows. The shaded conic and hemispheric areas indicate cones of fire from the various gun positions of the Flying Fortress. The smaller diagrams in the upper-left corner of this chart indicate the gas and oil tanks, and at the bottom, the various points of armor within the plane. The two circles indicate by cross hatching, the various over lapping of cones of fire, both from the front and from the rear of the plane. The diagrams in the upper left of the chart indicate the various gun positions. Note that this chart was current for the introduction of the B-17G with chin turrets.

Nazi pilots were instructed that the most vulnerable area of this airplane was the entire wing between the inboard engines. This is noted on the bottom right of the chart, beneath the tip of the wing w/ the star. A great deal of study went into this chart.

Another technique that helped make daylight bombing become more effective was the quality of the formation itself. Loose formations and isolated planes would attract German pilots for relatively easy kills, without paying too heavy a price. When all planes within a group formation flew in a tight arrangement, their target area would be more restricted and they would have a better fire concentration on the attacking fighter planes. A typical group was made up of four squadrons, and their planes would assemble in echelon formation with a lead plane and wingmen behind and to the right and left. The formation would be composed of a lead squadron—a high squadron to the right, and a low squadron to the left. Each of these squadrons would be developed with several echelons of planes, slightly staggered behind one another primarily to avoid prop wash and turbulence. This formation would be made up usually with 18 to 36 planes, depending on the target, the degree of the effort, and the availability of aircraft.

The major tactic that changed the odds and made daylight bombing devastating to Germany was the constant improvement of our fighter escort. In the early days of the war, our fighters had a limited range of about 300 miles. On my second mission to Brux, we flew over 600 miles just to reach the target. This meant that we had fighter escort from the English Channel to Frankfort, Germany, only half the distance to the synthetic oil refinery. The German fighter pilot knew this limitation and consequently would not engage or make an appearance until the last of

70 • "Know Thy Enemy"

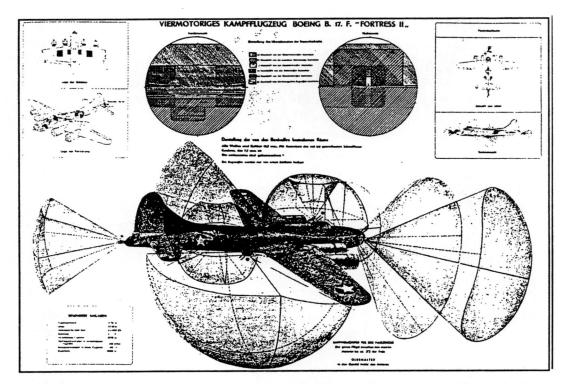

German chart used by Luftwaffe pilots to study B-17 cones of fire from 50 cal. machine guns and also the vulnerable areas of this flying fortress.

North American P-51 Mustang

Imperial War Museum-London

our escort were compelled to return to England because of limited fuel capacity. As soon as the last P-47, P-38, P-51 (and in some cases the British Spitfire) waggled their wings and turned toward the West, we could immediately expect our enemy to approach from all directions. They seldom disappointed us. They arrived in waves, all the way to the target. They would then break off to avoid their own devastating flak and leave us to the antiaircraft gunners surrounding the point of impact for our bombs. This reprieve from the German fighters was replaced with an equally potent weapon. They knew and we knew that we had no choice but to subject the formation of bombers to this barrage so that we could drop our bombs on the chosen target.

As soon as we left the flak behind us and headed for home, the first waves of fighters would again hit us. Most of these planes had time to land, rearm, and refuel. Their attack would continue until our own fighters would rendezvous with the bombers and individual dogfights would take place. As droppable wing tanks were developed, our fighters gradually extended their range until late in 1944 when they could go all the way to and from most targets in Europe. The P-51 Mustang became the best "Little Friend" of the the B-17s and B-24s.

Who were these German fighters that believed in their cause with the same determination as we did? I can honestly state that I never hated this enemy throughout my tour of duty. Our skirmishes were similar to the contests that I had experienced on the football field or the hockey rink. Each time I gave everything I owned to beat my opponent, but I never hated him. I expected my opponent to put forth his best effort in order to win. The many times when I saw falling bombers or fighters turning earthward, I could not let the individual inside these planes become too personal. My mind had steeled itself to not dwell on death associated with planes exploding or bombs being dropped on foreign cities. It was a contest in which goals had been set, rules developed, with an opposition trying to alter the results, with some participants being lucky, and with others the victims. This all looks and sounds unrealistic when you see these impersonal words strung together, but to daily partake in this foolish and stupid contest, one had to prepare mentally for the task assigned by outside forces. This same philosophy would also hold true for my enemy.

Early in the war, back in the late 1930s, the German JU87 dive bomber was the plane most responsible for the Nazi march across Europe. It was known as a STUKA. It was slow and clumsy, and it required complete control of the air space to be effective. The Battle of Britain determined the types of fighter planes that I would see in my phase of the war. The JU87 became obsolete.

72 • "Know Thy Enemy"

Messerschmitt ME-109

Focke-Wulf FW-190

The Me-109, the Messerschmitt, was Germany's first line fighter at the beginning of the war. It had a wing span of 32'6.5", a fuselage length of 29'4", a top speed of 400 mph, and a ceiling of 37,000 feet. The typical ME-109 was armed with eight .303 cal machine guns and a 30 mm cannon that fired through the propeller hub. This cannon, or "maschinenkanone," was designated the MK108 and was specifically designed as an anti-bomber cannon. The cannon was 41.6" long and weighed 127.87#. It fired a round that weighed 16.96 oz. at a rate of 850 rounds per minute. The muzzle velocity was low so that the fighters were forced to close into an effective range of under 500 yards, subjecting them to the defensive firepower of the bombers. Three or four rounds of the MK108 were usually enough to down a bomber, only one fifth of the number of 20mm shell hits needed.

The plane was most efficient above 20,000 feet, the altitude at which most of our bombing missions were flown. It had a fuel-injected engine that would not cut-out under negative Gs and it was a good steady gun platform from which to fire. The negative side of this constantly changing airplane was that it was fairly heavy on its controls and was not equipped for extra fuel drop tanks, which gave it limited air time endurance.

Another Messerschmitt plane we often encountered on bombing missions was the ME-110. It was classified as a long-range escort fighter and was known by the German Air Force as "Zerostorer" or destroyer. This twin engined plane with twin stabilizers carried two of the MK-108 cannons in its nose. It also had rocket launchers that would fire into bomber formations from outside of the B-17s machine gun range. It was a relatively easy target for our fighters, but it was very effective when unopposed.

One of the best fighter planes in World War II was the Focke-Wulf FW-190. It had a wing span of 34'-5", a fuselage length of 29', a top speed of 400 mph, a range of 525 miles, and a ceiling of 37,500 feet. Many of these planes were also armed with two 30mm MK-108 cannons, along with numerous machine guns. Special FW-190s were heavily armored and would actually ram B-17s in order to bring them down. If their plane was damaged too much to permit a return to their base, they would bail out over German territory. They believed the risk was worth the destruction of a B-17. Should our fighters catch one of these special FW-190 fighters, they would become an easy target because of their poor maneuverability and speed.

There were periods when we were without fighter cover and we would see over one hundred of the FW-190s attack in waves. It was always difficult to determine which model of German fighter was initiating an attack because they would be just a speck in the sky one second and then come by in a blur the next. Often they were so close that you could actually see the pilot. The rule that most crews used when there was any doubt: shoot at anything that points its nose at you. Sometimes a friendly fighter made this mistake and was fired upon. We knew that Germans had captured many of our planes that had to land behind enemy lines. They had no qualm about putting these planes in the sky for

74 • "Know Thy Enemy"

Messerschmitt ME-109

Messerschmitt ME-110 with rocket launchers

their own purposes, such as getting closer to bomber formations, getting information, and so forth.

Several other types of German planes that I had the fortune or misfortune of seeing were the ME-410 and the ME-262. The ME-410 was a twin engine and rather ugly fighter that was only seen on rare occasions. The ME-262, the first military jet fighter, hit the 95th Bomb Group late in my tour of duty. Our formation had a ME-262 make a front-end attack that carried him through our group of planes so fast that I don't believe a single shot was fired. This was even after one of our fighters warned us that they were in the area. The rate of closure was so fast that it was next to impossible to swing a gun on it. Few were ever shot down, even by our fighters. Many were destroyed on the ground, and it was fortunate that this new fighter was introduced very late in the war. Hitler wanted to make this plane into an attack bomber. As a result, it was too late to cause great destruction against our heavy bombers.

Shortly after the Allied fighter escort planes were equipped with droppable wing tanks and could escort the bombers to and from most targets, the German fighter became less of a threat. It was only on a rare occasion that one could break through and hit the formation. Sometimes they would pick on a straggler—a B-17 that was damaged and had to go it alone. Others would coordinate their attack between rendezvous of different American fighters when one group would not arrive when the previous group had to return to base. We were particularly alert when we noticed our "Little Friends" turn tail and head for home. If suddenly the sky was void of escort planes, we could almost count on being hit by German fighters.

The other huge danger that remained throughout the war was the intense fire power from flak batteries. These radar-directed heavy anti-aircraft guns were usually one of the following: the 88mm Flak 41, the 105mm Flak 38, or the 128mm Flak 40 guns. As an example of the size of the shell that they threw up at us, the 128mm shell weighed 87.3 pounds, had a muzzle velocity of 2,886 ft. per second, and could be fired at the rate of 10 rounds per minute reaching an altitude of 48,556 feet.

The standard radar used with AA guns surrounding German targets was the"Wurzburg-D," which had a tracking range of 15 miles. With this kind of equipment, our formations of bombers could be picked up at the I. P. point, where we turned in for our bombing run, approximately six or seven miles from the target, and still track us for several minutes after bombs away. The Germans knew that we would fly straight and level during the bomb run, and they would put up a barrage of shells that would box in the entire length of this critical flight path. It was awesome.

Each target, depending on its importance to the war effort or probability of attack, had a dozen or more flak batteries surrounding it. Each flak battery consisted of six to eight guns, mostly 88mm and 105 mm. Some cities had railroad flak batteries that usually had four 105 mm guns that were also radar controlled. These could be moved as needed.

A typical German "Gross battery" of AA guns was made up of three or four batteries placed around a command post facing the priority direction from which bombers could be expected to attack. Near the command post were

76 • "Know Thy Enemy"

Formation of ME-410s

German Jet Fighter ME-262

two radar sets with their own power generator units. This design was developed in order to produce the maximum possible weight of aimed fire power against British night bomber streams and American Eight Air Force day bomber formations.

As the war moved through 1944, the German fighter plane became less of a factor and the reverse was true of the anti-aircraft technology.

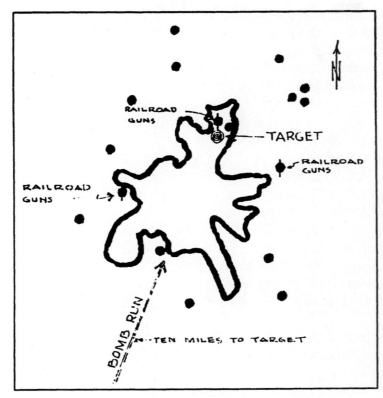

Magdeburg, Germany flak map. Each black dot represents one flak battery of eight guns. The three black dots with lines through them represents railroad flak batteries with four guns each. The bomb run for June 29, 1944 is indicated. 124 guns would be aimed at the B-17s this day.

German 105mm flak gun

Better radar was developed, early warning systems improved, and, of course, the vast experience of the observers and gunners on the ground from the practice we gave them.

Some missions that carried me to important German targets had a wall of flak so intense that we were flying through dense smoke for several minutes with little or no visibility. Shell fragments would hit the planes and sound like hail. Other pieces would find their way through the thin aluminum skin of our B-17s, sometimes finding a piece of equipment to damage, like an engine, gas tank, or oxygen system. At other times, they would hit a crew member. These small pieces of flak could do an unbelievable amount of damage because they would spin like a bundle of razor blades. A small fragment hitting our gas tanks usually would not create too much of a problem, since the tanks of B-17s were self-sealing for small holes. A one-quarter inch piece of spinning flak could tear off an arm. A direct hit from a shell would blow the plane out of the sky. Many fragments would hit a main spare in a wing and remove it. Others could knock an engine off its mountings or blow the tail section off.

The B-17 was a tough plane and could sustain an unbelievable amount of damage. Many planes returned to Base with large sections missing, with whole systems made inoperative, and of course with wounded or killed crew members. A direct hit in the gas tank or bomb bay created an instant explosion with all crew members doomed. Flak was our worst enemy because there was no way any of us could fight back. We had to ride it out, regardless of its intensity.

Despite all of the destructive power that the Germans released on us, I never held any animosity or resentment toward any individual. By the same token, I never had any deep feelings about dropping 6,000 pounds of bombs on a target nor, as on some occasions, when we toggled out bombs one at a time across the breadth of a German City in retaliation for similar raids on England. War isn't suppose to make sense. By definition it is the act of exerting violence or force against another. It has never resolved anything in proportion to its cost in lives or property. Each generation has to learn this truth.

 D-Day June 6, 1944

For the past week, a ripple of rumors had kept creeping through the 95th B.G. There had been hints that the invasion of Europe was about to take place, but no one was quite sure when and where this event would actually occur. Various individuals were sure that the landings would happen at hundreds of different locations along the jagged thousands of miles of coastline. Most, however, believed that it would be somewhere in the Pas-de-Calais area of France.

Targets across the English Channel at its narrowest point, such as Boulogne, Calais and Le-Touguet, were hit each day for the past several weeks by our Group and other Allied bombers. We did not know at this time, nor did the German High Command, that the sole purpose of this constant attention and effort on this portion of the French coast was meant to give the impression that the eminent invasion would take place there.

We enjoyed hitting these targets because each could be classified as a "milk run" or easy mission. You would get credit for a mission, have minimal flak exposure, and had only a slight probability of seeing enemy aircraft. However, at this period in my tour of duty, I had been assigned as a squadron lead navigator. This meant that lead navigators were usually not assigned to this type of mission, but rather to more distant targets deep in Germany.

The only flight that I did have to the Pas-de-Calais area was on June 4th, my 9th mission. We hit a target on the coast near the small city of Boulogne. As we approached our target from the northwest, we actually released our bombs while over the English Channel. . . . .the momentum of our formation threw the bombs forward in a lazy arc to the target area. We immediately turned away to the south and some of the planes on the inside of this maneuver were never actually over land. By far, this would be my easiest mission for which I would receive credit.

Late on the evening of June 5th, I found my name on the board that scheduled me for a mission the next day. I was elated to fly so soon and was looking forward to another "milk run." By the number of crews selected for this flight, it became apparent that it was to be a maximum effort, especially when we read that other personnel were ordered to standby for the possibility of a second target to be hit by another contingent from our Group. This, we all knew, was not standard procedure so a certain uneasiness crept into our conversations on the long walk back to our barracks.

The next morning when they came to get the crews out of the sack, there was an air of something important about to happen. As each of us dressed and walked toward the mess hall, it was very obvious that this day would be different. Instead of the usual slow shuffle in almost total silence through the early English morning mist, each airman wanted to talk. There was an excitement in all of the overlapping conversations going on. Today, each officer was verbally expressing the many thoughts that were usually suppressed on all other trips to this same mess hall.

In the excitement, some of the men even dished up, ate, and enjoyed the powdered scrambled "green eggs." This fact only becomes relevant when you know that crews going on actual combat missions could have farm fresh eggs fixed anyway they desired. This could be equated to an infantry man clapping with glee when served Spam, or any person in the Pacific being dished up the famous Australian "mutton."

The same cautious enthusiasm was on the faces of the cooks and mess personal that waited on us. This early morning detail was considered a "crap" assignment and was usually expressed in their zombie like attitudes as they prepared and dished out the three A.M. breakfast. Not this morning, it was as if they knew something that the flight crews were only guessing about.

The walk from the officers mess to the briefing room seemed shorter than usual. Enlisted men began joining our approach to the one room that would expose today's destination. They were also aware that this was not just another mission, but one with some special significance. It was also noticeable that the vehicular traffic darting about was several times the normal amount.

Inside the briefing room, the atmosphere was electrifying because the noise level had an unreal crescendo to it; the smoke from cigars and cigarettes was unusually thick, as well as the noticeable uneasiness of each crew member. The only thing that had not changed was the appearance of the front wall of the room. The opaque dull drape was still pulled over the important map of continental Europe, concealing the information from each flier. Today, a member of the briefing crew was guarding this secret by being sure no one got near the curtain and had a sneak preview of our target. We would not have long to wait, however.

When Colonel Carl Truesdell, Jr. and his entourage entered the room, everyone "popped to attention" in perfect unison. I had never witnessed this type of proficiency in the briefing room prior to a mission. Someone in the group before us yelled "at ease" and the entire audience dropped their butts as one.

Before he could speak, Colonel Truesdell had to remove the usual cigar from his mouth and then, with a calmness that somehow he was able to muster, he started the briefing with these words "Gentlemen, this is it." "Today, the Allied Forces are about to invade Europe and the 95th Bomb Group will take part in this momentous occasion." Now, all that we needed to know was where.

The curtain was pulled back and the target and invasion area was exposed. It was not on the coast in the Pas de Calais area as most of us had guessed, but rather that part of France that was south of England between Cherbourg and LeHavre. As we got a very detailed explanation of what was about to take place, we could immediately grasp the logic that determined the location of the invasion. At the very moment we were hearing about the operation, we were told that it actually had started many hours before. Thousands of ships and boats of every description had sailed from hundreds of English ports and were approaching the French coast as we listened with absolute attention. Other forces, besides the air arm, were now about to join us in defeating the German occupation of Europe.

The map at the front of the room only indicated the details of our trip to the target and the route that we would take to return to England. It was not much different from other missions at first glance. Several other officers on the briefing team went into enough details about the operation that would make June 6th an unforgettable day, one that we knew was not going to be a typical combat mission.

The importance of the selection of this part of France was made obvious when we were told that the entire Cherbourg Peninsula was a high priority so that millions of tons of supplies and equipment could be landed and stored for the days ahead. Other beachheads would be taken and the troops would fan out in all directions, taking as much territory as quickly as possible. Men of the Allied Forces had been secretly preparing themselves for this day, and we were assured that they were ready.

We were shown charts that gave the big picture of the air operation. Thousands of bombers and a similar number of fighter planes would be in the skies at the same time. The traffic problems were tremendous. Each plane and Group had to be accounted for and a detailed and very specific flow of planes to and from the invasion area had been worked out. The bombers had routes that required all three Air Divisions from the Eighth Air Force to flow from hundreds of air fields in East Anglia to the invasion front, and then to divert around Cherbourg in a clockwise direction.

82 • D-Day June 6, 1944

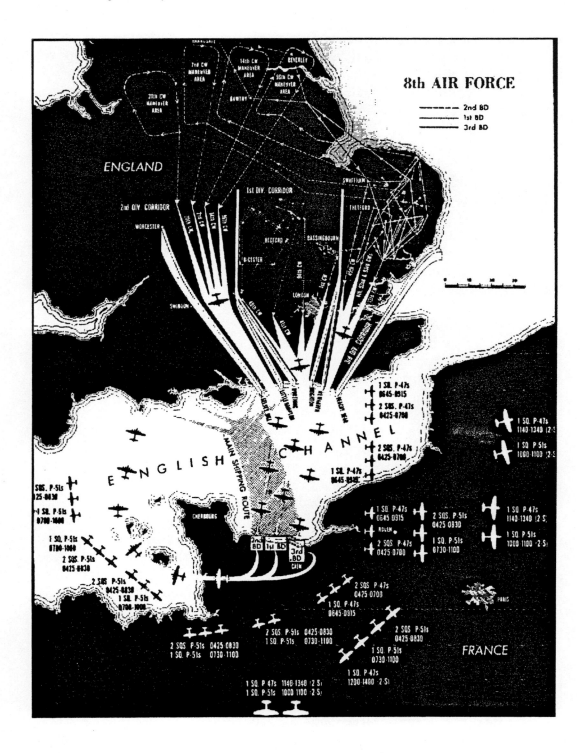

About this time each of the excited airmen in this briefing room received a printed message from the Supreme Commander of The Allied Forces, General Dwight David Eisenhower. The following is the message that every member of the various branches of the service and support units received:

> Soldiers, sailors, and airmen of the Allied Expeditionary Force. You are about to embark upon the great crusade, toward which we have striven these many months. The eyes of the world are upon you. The hopes and prayers of liberty-loving people everywhere march with you. In company with our brave allies and brothers in arms on other fronts, you will bring about the destruction of the German war machine, the elimination of Nazi tyranny over the oppressed peoples of Europe, and security for ourselves in a free world. Your task will not be an easy one. Your enemy is well trained, well equipped and battle hardened. He will fight savagely. But this is the year 1944! Much has happened since the Nazi triumphs of 1940-41. The United Nations have inflicted upon the Germans great defeats in open battle, man to man. Our air offensive has seriously reduced their strength in the air and their capacity to wage war on the ground.
>
> Our home fronts have given us an overwhelming superiority in weapons and munitions of war, and placed at our disposal great reserves of trained fighting men. The tide has turned! The free men of the world are marching together to victory!
>
> I have full confidence in your courage, devotion to duty and skill in battle. We will accept nothing less than full victory!
>
> Good luck! And let us beseech the blessing of Almighty God upon this great and noble undertaking.

(Note: The order was distributed to assault elements after their embarkation. It was read by commanders to all other troops in the Allied Expeditionary Force. I received a printed copy of this same Order from General Eisenhower.)

A few hours after Eisenhower's Order of the Day was made known, President Roosevelt led the American people in prayer:

> "Almighty God: Our sons, pride of our Nation, this day have set out upon a mighty endeavor, a struggle to preserve our Republic, our religion, and our civilization and to set free a suffering humanity........."

The feeling I felt at this moment was like being on a football team that was leading the conference and we were about to take the field for a game that would decide the National Championship. I felt ready and prepared as I knew each participant did. By the same token, each knew that unknown dangers lurked ahead and that the cost was bound to be high.

The 95th Bomb Group had a target at Arqentan, just south of Caen, France. As we crossed the invasion coastline, British troops were embarking from the bowels of a galaxy of ships of different sizes and shapes. Men were wading ashore simultaneously along the entire length of this selected French coast. The Americans landed on Utah and Omaha beachheads and the British and Canadian troops approached the Gold, Juno, and Sword beachheads. The actual attack of this memorable day was accomplished with 176,475 men, 20,111 vehicles, 1,500 tanks and 12,000 planes. The planning to invade the Normandy Beaches was known as "Operation Overlord."

The briefing we received this morning, June 6th, included the usual information that we were given for any other target, with the one exception. For the first time, we were told to look for anything unusual that the Germans might throw at us. They knew that an invasion of the Continent was inevitable, so it was expected that they might have a secret weapon that had been held back just for this occasion. This information, in all of its vagueness, only added to our apprehension. Would we be vaporized? Would they have a new and more deadly type of flak? Did they have something that would make our engines quit running? These were some of the rumors that we heard on the way to our hardstands and our B-17s prior to take off.

Everything about our briefing and this day seemed to be special. I can remember listening to the pilot and copilot run through the "check list" before starting engines. One would read the list while the other repeated each action. Green flare at 0500 hours. "Start engines"; "Fire guard posted"—"Fire guard posted"; "Batteries on"—"Batteries on"; "Hydraulic pump auto"—"Hydraulic pump auto": "Hydraulic pressure up"—"Hydraulic pressure up"; "Flaps up"—"Flaps up"; "Cowl flaps open"—"Cowl flaps open", "Master switch on"—"Master switch on"; "Gyros caged"—"Gyros caged"; "Bomb bay doors closed"; "Bomb bay doors closed"—"Start number one." It was now that we heard the usual whine and sputter before the engine kicked off with a roar. Each of the four Pratt & Whitney engines were started in a specific sequence.

As each engine coughed to a start, a new set of checklist items had to be run through and repeated. "Booster pump on. Throttle cracked. Fuel mixture to idle cut-off. Prop high rpm. Magnetos off. Circuit breakers on. Generators on. Starter on for 20 seconds. Ignition. Prime the pump." Then and only then, would No. 1 engine come alive.

Immediately, a new set of instructions would flow out. "Mixture to auto-rich. Check oil-pressure. Stabilize at 1,000 rpm. Check fuel pressure." Like the previous instructions, these also had to be verified by concurring that the action was indeed taken care of. Oil and cylinder head temperatures on each of the four gauges had to ascend into the green arc.

"Wheel chocks locks out." Flight controls locks off." "Flight control locks off, exercise controls." "Radio on and set."

Another flare from the control tower meant that it was time to taxi. The right hand of the first pilot was placed over the four throttles and slowly he pushed the two outside or outboard throttles forward and the 65,000 pound bomber lumbered out of the hardstand toward the perimeter runway.

The left throttle was pulled back and the right throttle was pushed forward. The pilot applied left rudder and a small amount of left brake with his toe. Tires squealed as the B-17 turned sharply to the left onto the perimeter track. All around this huge field, 34 planes were lining up so that they could be ready to take off in a predetermined sequence. The squeal of these many tires against the pavement almost made you feel that you were on a pig farm in Iowa. Each plane was parked slightly askew of the one ahead of it for better observation and then the parking brake was pressed on.

Finally, the order was given for the actual take-off. "Tail wheel locked. Parking brake off; Cowl flaps trail. . . . flaps up; take-off." The brakes were held as all four throttles were slowly moved forward to the fire stop. "Release brakes." The plane slowly moved forward down the 7,000 foot main runway, just 30 seconds behind the B-17 in front and 30 seconds before the plane behind. Then the increasing speed was called out in miles per hour by tens: 40-50-60, etc., until 110 mph was reached. The red lights near the end of the runway let you know that it was time to lift off. Wheels up—Climb at 500 feet per minute and hold airspeed at 125 mph.

About this time each crew member checked in on their intercom, and at 10,000 feet each was told to get on oxygen. The power was reduced to 30 inches of manifold pressure and 2,000 rpm. Now, it was essential to hold a predetermined heading, rate of climb, and airspeed to avoid running into one another, especially if confronted with several thousand feet of cloud cover.

Each time we took off, the same ritual took place. Today, though, it seemed more meaningful for some reason. The thought raced through my mind that we had ten men, each trained to do precise duties on this complex flying fortress. Only a few months before, we were scattered around the United States doing ten different jobs. Remarkable!

This was a maximum effort with 34 of our planes in the 95th formation. The 100th and the 390th Bomb Groups each had similar numbers so that the 13th Combat Wing would leave England today 100 plus strong. On this day I was squadron navigator of the high element in the formation. The take-off and rendezvous with the 390th and the 100th B.G. was routine. This particular day near perfect assembly was required because of the total air activity going on all over Southern England, particularly in East Anglia. With the entire Eighth Air Force, both bombers and fighter aircraft, plus the entire British contingent, it made the skies very active. The fact that these formations had targets to hit in a limited area and at about the same time made the logistics for this operation most important.

The following actual combat map for the 6th of June indicates the route of the 95th B.G. We left England near Eastbourne at about 15,000 ft altitude, which is a relatively low bombing altitude. This height would make the actual bombing results more accurate, something that would be imperative for this operation. Our course across the English Channel was south southwest (190 degrees) to a point just west of LeHavre. It was at this point that we altered course to a heading of 182 degrees for our run into the target, which was a concentration of German troops and supplies.

The only unusual observation, one that would prove to be different from previous missions, was hundreds of vertical contrail-like plumes of white smoke that rose thousands of feet above us. This phenomenon took place only on June 6th, something I had not seen nor would see again. These parallel white columns of smoke looked like a huge wall made of vertical bars. Our wings cut through these nebulous, vague columns of mist, just like we were trying to escape from a giant bird cage. It was an eerie feeling, especially since we were told at briefing to expect the Germans to use new and different types of weapons if the Allies attempted an invasion. This was certainly different, but it was something that did not appear to have negative results. If this was a secret weapon, we could live with it.

Nothing further transpired, however, and we continued on our target run and dumped our load of bombs. Just south of the target, a distance of about 30 miles or about 5 minutes elapsed time, we turned at the R.P. Point to a heading of 295 degrees. This took us just south of Rochefort, France, and over the Bay of Biscay.

We altered course slightly to avoid the Channel Islands of Jersey and Guernsey, where we knew that we could pick up some flak. Once we crossed the English coast near Weymouth, we turned on a heading of 52 degrees, which would take us to our base at Horham.

This day required flying the exact route that had been predetermined. With thousands of planes taking part in this operation in such a limited space, there was no room for error. If any plane deviated from the explicit orders and direction then, they would chance being shot out of the sky by Allied fighter planes. The Germans had many of our captured planes and could create havoc should they intermingle with our units in this operation.

When we flew over the Channel, we could see thousands of ships of every size; they were making unusual patterns on the water surface.

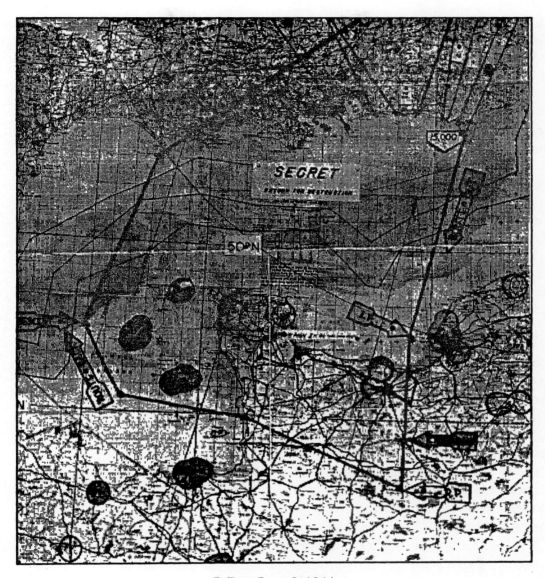

D-Day June 6, 1944
Mission by 95th B.G.

This was BIG and we all knew it. Yes, we were a part of history. For the first time, we could actually see how our Group fit into the whole picture. For nearly two years planes from the Bomber Command flew to isolated targets and unloaded their bombs, but never actually saw how this affected the total war effort. All these missions would begin to tell now that the German army and air force had to face the effort being put forth by the rest of the world. We had destroyed bridges, knocked out rail lines, blown up factories, desolated their air force, depleted their oil and gas supplies, put their cities in ruin, and lowered the general moral of the German people to the point of being ineffectual.

This mission on June 6th was designated Field Order Number 394 by the Eighth Airforce and it would be Sorty Number 145 for the 95th B.G. Two more flights of bombers would leave our base this day to assist our friends and brothers who were fighting on the ground in France. We knew their job would be rough and that they could use all of the help that we could give them.

The flight today was my 10th credited mission, and immediately thereafter, I was given a four-day pass to go to London. The excitement in this famous old city equaled my own inner feelings. London had tasted war for over five years and its people now knew that we were about to give the enemy the realization that no one wins in such a conflict.

It was next to impossible to go into a pub and buy a drink. If you were in uniform, there was someone who insisted that they treat you to a "bitter" or "mild." I was proud to be an American, but I shall never forget the pride and fortitude of the British people. They had endured so much and complained so little. I don't know of another people like them.

Several times while on this leave, I almost got my head knocked off by various paratroopers who had just returned from the front. Fortunately, they were looking for any American airman from the 9th Airforce. It seems that many of the pilots from the 9th who dropped paratroopers or who towed gliders into France got "chicken" at the last minute and got rid of their cargo prematurely, often in swamps and marshes. Many Americans were shot dangling from their chutes that were caught up in trees or had to wade waste deep in a swamp. I saw many 9th Airforce officers with black eyes, cut-up faces, or torn uniforms. I also saw many paratroopers being incarcerated by pairs of M. P.s. Thank God, I had on the right shoulder patch, a large gold 8 with wings on a blue background.

We had gained a foothold in Europe; something Hitler never believed possible. You could not help but feel a sense of accomplishment whenever you realized that you had just done the impossible.

The No-Ball Target

Tuesday evening, on July 5th, I received the news that I was scheduled to fly a mission tomorrow. This particular mission would put me over the halfway point on my tour of duty, with seventeen to go and eighteen behind me. It may sound simplistic to put importance on how many credited missions one flew over Europe, but when all of the dust settles, life and death depended on these numbers. Fate, of course, also played a hand in the outcome of this game of roulette.

The briefing, early Wednesday morning, brought a huge smile to my face. Our target today was a "No-Ball Target," even though it was announced as a tactical mission. My smile was motivated by the knowledge that this trip would be a short duration to the coast of France and that it was likely that we would not be hit by German fighters. We could get over and away from the target area before the fighters could rise to meet us, plus we would have more than adequate escort help from our "Little Friends."

In the past, I had missed out on many of these "no-ball targets" because it was the policy of our and other groups to eliminate navigators from all but the lead crew. Since these missions were close to the coast of England, it was felt that a navigator was not necessary for each B-17 in trouble to find their way back to its Base. This type of special tactical mission was designed to hit unusual targets along the coast of the Netherlands, Belgium, and France. "No-Ball" was a code name given by the Allies for Germany's secret weapon that they called "VERGEITUNG, 1" or that became known simply as the V-1.

The sites consisted of a huge inclined ramp and many special structures in a complex. The British R.A.F. had been hitting these sites for over a year, not completely knowing their entire function. Intelligence and constant photographs kept the Allies informed on the progress of this weapon that the Germans were obviously depending on. On June 13th, London had the unfortunate opportunity to be the first target for the very first "Buzz Bomb"; and on this day, the "Second Battle of London" began. There were approximately 38 launching sites along the European coast of the English Channel and their inclined ramps were

90 • The No-Ball Target

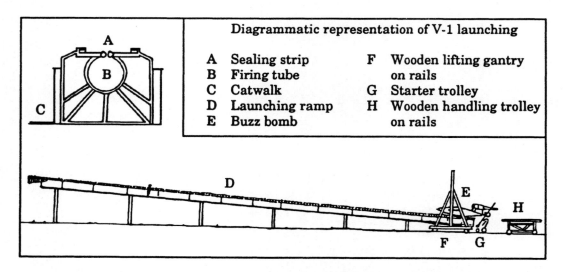

Detail of typical V-1 launching ramps—Scale: 1″=40 feet

V-1 in actual flight

primarily directed toward London and in some cases other important English cities.

I had my very first opportunity to fly on one of these missions once I became a lead navigator. I had become very envious of the other crew members because of the numerous "easy" missions that they got credit for, a timely overture that was not extended to yours truly and other navigators. On June 24th, when I was briefed to go to the coast of France, I learned a great deal about the difficulty of identifying these targets. The Germans cleverly hid them in the midst of farm yards, orchards, small villages, and so forth. This particular day we went on to hit an alternate target inland because the V-1 site became obscured by clouds and could not be positively identified. Today our briefing was complete with very detailed photographs that had been taken by reconnaissance planes of the 8th A.F. or from British de Havilland Mosquitoes. Each of these launching sites were given specific numbers by the Allies, such as Ailly-le-Vieux-Claher, France, was always referred to as No-Ball 27, which was our target this day. The blow-up of some of the photos indicated key structures and, of course, the ever present concrete ramp. The ramp was approximately 215 feet long and about 12 feet wide.

A ramp this size may appear to be obvious from an altitude of 12,000 feet (about half our normal bombing height), but the Germans placed these structures under large trees and other forms of camouflage. To find them on a bomb run required good eyes, clear weather, and luck.

I was happy for this "milk-run" type mission for another reason. On June 16th, I got my second pass to go to London. "Waddy," "Weak," and I left on Thursday and stayed in this famous city until Sunday afternoon. Besides spending all our daylight hours visiting most of the historical sights in the world's largest city, we were exposed to air raid sirens and alerts day and night. The first wave of V-1s started coming over. The first V-1 actually hit London just three days before, on June 13th. On the 16th, the Germans started sending their "Retaliation Weapon V-1" across the Channel to begin a desperate effort to alter the outcome of the war.

No one on the streets of London knew anything about this different type of bomb. They learned in a hurry that they could hear a buzzing sound, like an old car going up a steep hill, and that they could actually get glimpses of this pilotless plane flying over head. These planes were at an altitude of about 2,000 feet and could be spotted over the rooftops. The other unique thing that each of us soon learned was the fact that 12 or 14 seconds after the buzzing sound ceased, the missile dove earthward and exploded into a structure. Since this V-1 carried a bomb weighing approximately one ton, it created a great deal of havoc. You soon learned by the sound and the sight of one of these flying bombs passing

92 • The No-Ball Target

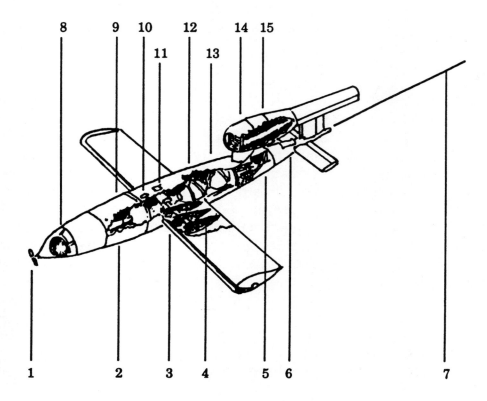

**Internal details of a Type L flying bomb.
V-1 or "Buzz Bomb"**

KEY
1. Air log to determine length of flight
2. War head
3. Cable cutter (optional, one or two forms)
4. Wooden ribs on tubular spar (some were metal)
5. Battery, fuel and guidance controls
6. Pneumatic motors to operate controls
7. 400-foot aerial for ranging transmitter
8. Compass to control gyros for guidance, enclosed in wooden sphere.
9. Twin fuse pockets in horizontal main fuse
10. Fuel filler cap
11. Lifting lug
12. Fuel tank
13. Compressed air spheres for pneumatic control motors
14. Jet motor flanked by mixing venturis
15. Combustion chamber

in a certain direction that you would not become a statistic for the moment. It was the "buzz-bomb" that you could not see or perhaps could not hear that might be the one that landed in your vicinity.

The British did not know during these early days just how to attack this new monster. They placed large balloons with dangling steel cables on the east and south sides of London in order to intercept these incoming V-ls. Their guns fired from within the city. None of this was practical because a lucky hit would only alter the course of the missile and send it to a building still within the city. London covered an area of over 100 square miles, which was a choice target for a bomb that could not be aimed very accurately.

Within a week or two, the British moved these balloons and gun emplacements to the coast. At the same time, the British R.A.F. started to develop techniques to destroy these flying bombs. Their fighter planes patroled the Channel to intercept the incoming V-ls. They tried various ways and angles of attack in order to shoot down this 400 mph small target. Some pilots discovered that they could tip or upset the V-1's gyros by diving in front of the missile and creating a turbulence from their prop wash. Some used the method of flying along side and placing their wing below the short stubby wing of the V-1. This would roll them over, tip the V-1, upset the important gyros, and send it diving into the sea.

The fighter planes that proved to be the most effective against these fast moving targets were the following planes: the British Hawker "Tempest"; the Spitfire; and the Gloster Metior "Jettie"; and also the American P-51 "Mustang." At night, the British de Havilland "Mosquito" and the American P-61 "Black Widow" proved most effective. By August 1944, the German attacks were reaching their zenith. In a 24-hour period during the height of the launchings, 316 V-ls were aimed toward southern England. Twenty-five of these bombs crashed at the launching site, 107 crossed the English coast, and 184 were shot down or destroyed.

In July 1944, 2441 people were killed while another 7101 were wounded. These casualties were incurred despite the fact that only 50 percent reached the English mainland. The launch sites built in the Cherburg area of France never were used because of the invasion on D-Day. After August, the advancing Allied forces captured most of the sites and terminated their destructive use. On September 6th, 1944, the Minister of Home Security, Mr. Herbert Morrison, announced to the British people, "The Battle Of London Is Won." The very next day a new phase started. On September 7th, the German "Retaliation Weapon Number 2, VERGELTUNG 2" was launched. The Allies soon referred to this even deadlier weapon as the V-2. (This weapon will be described later in some detail.)

London, a large and important target, was referred to by the Germans as "Targeet 42." During my first visit and first day, London had 150 V-1s launched at it, with 73 actually reaching the city. Eleven had been shot down, but of course exploded within this huge target. The first night, while "Waddy," "Weak," and I were out pubbing, a Buzz Bomb landed near enough to our hotel that it blew out all of the glass in our three large windows. There wasn't a square inch in our room that did not have jagged pieces of broken glass on it. Hip Hip Hurray for bitters and milds.

Just what was this V-1 FZG 76 pilotless bomb? The Germans started work on the retaliation weapon back in 1933, and it took the next ten years to perfect it. By June 13th, the Germans were ready to rain these missiles down on the population of England. Wernher von Braun worked with other German scientists to develop the V-1, the V-2, and other equally potent weapons, such as the Reichenberg Series. Table 2 contains some interesting statistics about this weapon. (It might be important to know that the United States was developing a similar flying bomb at the same time. It was known as FORD JB-2 and called the "LOON.")

The V-1 came abruptly to an end, and the V-2 immediately took over. The V-2s new weapon was an entirely different beast because it traveled almost vertically and returned to earth at a speed greater than the speed of sound. The V-2 was very inaccurate, but it arrived at its target without any warning. At its peak, around February 1945, 116 hit the London area. England received over 1100 V-2s with London getting about one-half. As the Allies advanced, other European cities and troops also became targets.

Our no-ball target, on this Wednesday, was a V-1 site that we plastered with the bombs from the 26 B-17s of the 95th B. G. Six of our planes received severe battle damage from the intense flak that was thrown up. It was a usual greeting because the Germans recognized that this site would become a prime target for the Allies. This was a last ditch effort on the part of the Nazis and many of their AA guns were moved away from destroyed areas to these new launch sites. Even with excellent bombing results, the Germans, with the help of slave labor, could get these relatively simple ramps, pads and facilities back into operation within a few weeks. Our effort was merely a token endeavor to do whatever could be done to help London. The advancing Allied armies were the greatest deterrent.

If the Germans had put these "Rumpelkammes," the Nazi code name for the V-1 and V-2, into operation a year earlier, victory over Hitler and his fanatical plans might have been impossible. Today, these weapons are primitive and archaic. Now we have the capability of destroying the world, the billions of people in it, all living creatures, and everything that gives quality of life. One American fighter-bomber carries enough fire power today to equal all of the bombs dropped by both sides in World War II. If man could rechannel these resources (i.e., the expenditures and the knowledge), most of the problems of the world could be resolved. To this date, we are still on a collision course with Armageddon, perhaps not from the USSR, but certain other irresponsible countries with this capability.

Table 2—Statistics About V-1

VERGEITUNG-1	V-1 FZG 76
wing span	17'-4"
length	25'-4"
fuselage dia.	2'-9"
engine dia.	1'-10"
weight of bomb	1870 pounds
motor	Argus As 109-014 Rohe w/ 770# thrust
speed	400 mph
ceiling	8840 feet
total weight	4796 pounds

The V-1 is simple in concept. The following are the various sections of this pilotless plane-bomb:

NOSE SECTION
Formed of an aluminum alloy cone. It has a small propeller that governs the length of flight. When it spins out, the robot re-sets the controls from a flying position into a dive.

WARHEAD SECTION
Behind a bulkhead is the warhead of "Amatol" high-blast explosive. It has two impact switches, one on the nose and one on the bottom, in case it slides in.

MID SECTION
Fuel tank w/ weight of 1133 pounds. This section has a lifting lug to handle these units at the launch site.

FOURTH SECTION
Contains two pairs of spherical compressed air bottles, each with 900#/sq."

FIFTH SECTION
"Sleurgerat" - master and secondary gyros, fuel control mechanism, multiple dry-batteries to operate the electrical service.

FINAL FUSELAGE SECTION
The pneumatic servo-motors powered by compressed air.

The No-Ball Target

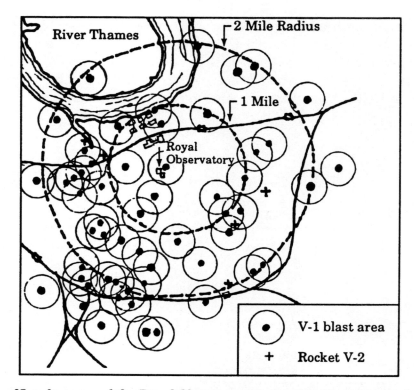

A section of London around the Royal Observatory indicating the extent and saturation of flying bombs. It shows both V-1 and V-2 impact areas. The entire area in this diagram is approximately 12 square miles. Note the number of bombs that hit certain spots near the observatory.

History of the V-1s that left Europe (Many of these bombs exploded at lauch site)	
Number of bombs to approach coast:	6,725
Casualties (approximate):	
Killed:	5,500
Injured:	18,000
Houses destroyed:	23,000
Number destroyed:	
By anti-aircraft guns:	1,859
By fighter planes:	1,846
By balloons:	230
First bomb to cross English coast:	13 June 1944
Last bomb to cross English coast:	29 March 1945
Maximum number destroyed by guns in single day:	68
Successful night interceptions by fighter planes:	142
Number of public air-raid warnings sounded:	402

		ALERTS	MISSILES HEARD
June			
16	Friday	5	17
17	Saturday	5	18
18	Sunday	4	19
19	Monday	7	21
20	Tuesday	5	3
21	Wednesday	3	5
22	Thursday	6	47
23	Friday	9	10
24	Saturday	4	7
25	Sunday	3	1
26	Monday	2	0
27	Tuesday	11	2
28	Wednesday	13	3
29	Thursday	9	9
30	Friday	11	7

This table indicates the number of missiles spotted by just one observer in London for the month of June, 1944.

V-1

Number of bombs to approach coast:	6,725
Casualties (approx.):	
Killed:	5,500
Injured:	18,000
Houses destroyed:	23,000
Number launched in first twenty-four hours:	155
Number launched on worst day (2 August):	316
Approximate cost:	£120
Number destroyed	
by anti-aircraft guns:	1,859
by fighters:	1,846
by balloons (approx.):	230
Maximum number destroyed by guns in single day:	68
Successful night interceptions by fighters:	142
Maximum number of anti-aircraft guns deployed; (3.7 in.):	542
(40mm):	503
Number of guns deployed in Diver Box;	
(3.7in.):	136
(40mm):	210
(20mm):	410
First bomb to cross coast:	13 June 1944
Last bomb to cross coast:	29 March 1945
Number of public air-raid warnings sounded:	402

History of the V-1s that left Europe. Many of these bombs exploded at launch site.
(Imperial War Museum-London)

98 • The No-Ball Target

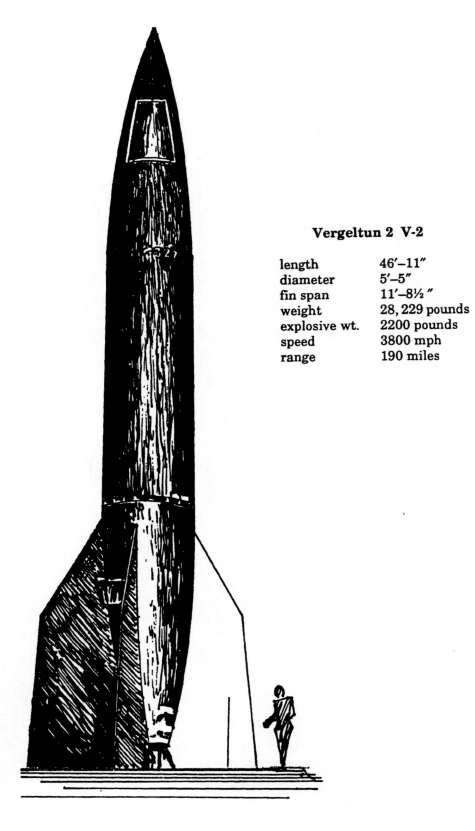

Vergeltun 2 V-2

length	46'–11"
diameter	5'–5"
fin span	11'–8½"
weight	28,229 pounds
explosive wt.	2200 pounds
speed	3800 mph
range	190 miles

Plane No. 297334

Most of the B-17s that flew in combat were either Model Fs or Gs. Though they appeared to be similar, to each crew member their plane had a special significance. Their affection to this functional aircraft was expressed by giving their "baby" a name and usually applying "nose art" on each side of the forward section. The plane that had this attraction for me was the first B-17 that our crew was issued. Because I became a lead navigator after my ninth mission, I only flew in this plane for eight of my total of 35 missions. By chance, these eight trips over Europe turned out to be more than any other crew member. The following is her history.

I have not been able to find the exact date this particular B-17 G rolled off the assembly lines at the Boeing Aircraft Plant in Seattle, Washington. However, it was accepted by the Air Force on March 1, 1944. The following chronological history of this plane would be fairly indicative of a heavy bomber in any Group:

March 1, 1944	B-17 No. 297334 accepted by Air Force.
March 17, 1944	The Lt. Cobb Crew was assigned this new aircraft at Grand Island, Nebraska.
April 1, 1944	Left Grand Island for England and combat via Bangor, Maine; Laborador; Iceland; and finally Ireland.
April 10, 1944	Landed in Nutts Corner, Ireland. Plane was taken away from our crew and was to be reassigned to some base in England.
April 19, 1944	Discovered that the plane was sent to Horham, England and the 95th Bomb. Group. Have made an effort to reclaim her.
April 20, 1944	The first combat mission was a no-ball target #1OA flown by Lt. C.S. McCall and crew

Plane No. 297334

April 22, 1944	McCall and crew took plane to Hamm, Germany.
April 25, 1944	Lt. H. Filshko and crew flew to Dijon, France.
April 26, 1944	Lt. H. W. Slusser with crew went to Brunswick, Germany.
April 27, 1944	In the morning Lt. Slusser hit a no-ball target #7A and in the afternoon Lt. C. L. Snownden flew her to LeCulot, France.
April 29, 1944	Lt. J.H. Bullard and crew made the planes first trip to Berlin, Germany.
May 1, 1944	Lt. Slusser hit another no-ball target #120.
May 7, 1944	The plane started on a mission to Berlin but had to return because of a gunners illness.
May 9, 1944	My first combat mission on this plane. Flew with Lt. W. G. Wood and crew to Laon Anthies, France-an airfield.
May 11, 1944	Plane was designated a spare and was not needed for a mission to Liege, Germany.
May 12, 1944	My second mission and my second flight in this plane. This time I flew with Lt. Charlie Snowden and crew to Czechoslovakia; one of the longer missions.
May 13, 1944	My third mission with my original crew. Lt. Frank Cobb and the guys got their first taste of combat at Osnabruck, Germany.
May 19, 1944	Flew No. 4 to Berlin, Germany w/ Lt. Cobb.
May 20, 1944	Flew No. 5 to Brussels, Belgium with LT. Cobb and crew.
May 23, 1944	With our original crew we flew as a spare and had to return to base when no one aborted.

May 24, 1944	Plane again was a spare and returned to base. Lt. Cobb cracked up plane on landing, damaging right landing gear, nos. 3 and 4 engines, and right wing. Plane will be out of commission for some time. Cobb was demoted to co-pilot.
July 12, 1944	Airplane finally repaired. Lt. J.A. Cotner and crew took her to Munich, Germany.
July 16, 1944	Lt. C.L. Bodin and crew flew to Stuttgart, Germany. I flew my 23rd mission with them.
July 17, 1944	A tactical mission flown by the Charlie Bodin Crew.
July 18, 1944	Another tactical mission by Bodin crew.
July 19, 1944	Lt. Cotner and crew went to Schweinfurt, Germany.
July 24, 1944	Lt. Bodin flew w/ crew on a tactical mission.
July 25, 1944	Another tactical mission by Bodin crew.
July 28, 1944	Lt. J.L. Walker and his crew had a mission to Mersburg, Germany.
August 1, 1944	A tactical mission #13 by Walker crew.
August 2, 1944	Lt. P.E. Fiess flew her on a tactical mission.
August 3, 1944	Lt. W.R. Olney and crew flew a tactical mission.
August 4, 1944	Lt. V. Deckard and his crew went to Hamburg, Germany.
August 6, 1944	Deckard and crew went back to Germany; this time to Rahmel.
August 7, 1944	Deckard and his boys got to fly the Lady to Trzebinia.
August 8, 1944	Deckard and crew went to Buzau, Germany.

August 12, 1944	Lt. Deckard had a mission to Toulouse, France.
August 15, 1944	Lt. Walker w/ his crew flew a tactical mission.
August 16, 1944	The Walker crew went to Zeitz, Germany.
August 24, 1944	Lt. P. A. Kross and his crew flew to Ruhland, Germany.
August 26, 1944	Lt. R.F. Harvey flew a tactical mission.
August 27, 1944	Lt. W.L. Hanson was the 16th different pilot to fly the Lady. His crew went to Husum, Germany.
August 30, 1944	Lt. R.P. Harry's crew went to Bremen, Germany.
September 1, 1944	The Harvey crew flew a tactical mission.
September 3, 1944	Lt. Harvey and his crew flew their 35th mission in the Lady. I will fly my last mission on Sept. 5th and return to the States w/ the Harvey crew.
September 5, 1944	Lt. W.H. Hart flew to Stuttgart, Germany.
September 8, 1944	Hart and crew went to Mainz, Germany.
September 9, 1944	Lt. K.C. Melvin with his crew went to Dusseldorf, Germany.
September 11, 1944	On a mission to Ruhland, Germany, today our Lady met her end. Lt. V.R. Moring, the 20th different pilot to handle No. 297334, and his crew were shot down. At 12:20 hr. at 50° 40'N and 13° 20'E left the formation with the right wing on fire. The entire crew, on their eighth mission, was able to bail out, and all were taken prisoner. They were Lt. V.L. Mooring, pilot; Lt. C.R. Swanson, co-pilot; Lt. A.P. Janson, navigator; Lt. R.A. Woerke, bombardier; Sgt. C.P. Stein, top-turret; Sgt. F. Alvievto, radio operator; Sgt. T.H. Merriman, ball turret; Sgt. W.P. Martin, waist gunner; and Sgt. J.G. Weber, tail gunner. The entire crew spent the remainder of the war as P.O.W.s.

Come Fly With Me • 103

No. 297334-B-17 nicknamed by crew as HAARD LUCK.
Picture taken by Sgt. Ed Schmidt at Bangor, Maine,
April 2, 1944, on the way to England and combat.

Krueger standing
by rear of plane.

Original crew just before
leaving the United States.

Plane No. 297334

This plane flew 41 combat missions, mostly to Germany, and it went out four times as a spare and each time returned to base because no planes aborted. Most crews flew their own plane. No. 297334 was an exception for several reasons. First, our crew was broken up early because of problems with the first pilot and my removal because of my special duties. Second, an excellent ground crew kept this plane in exceptional condition, so many lead crews took her on missions.

Twenty different crews flew this plane in combat. Below is a list of the officers who piloted the Lady and the number of times each took her on a mission:

Name	Missions	Name	Missions
Lt. F.H. Cobb	5	Lt. P.E. Feiss	1
Lt. C.S. McCall	2	Lt. W.R. Olney	1
Lt. H. Filshko	1	Lt. V. Deckhard	5
Lt. H.W. Slusser	3	Lt. P.A. Kross	1
Lt. C.L. Snowden	2	Lt. R.F. Harvey	1
Lt. J.H. Bullard	1	Lt. R.P. Harry	1
Lt. W.G. Wood	1	Lt. W.H. Hart	2
Lt. J.A. Cotner	2	Lt. K.C. Melvin	1
Lt. C.L. Bodin	5	Lt. W.L. Hanson	1
Lt. J.L. Walker	4	Lt. V.R. Moring	1
*Lt. Lloyd O. Krueger	8	(As navigator)	

Note: The B-17's in the 95th Bomb Group flew 9528 Sorties with 287 planes taking part. The average life of these planes was 33.2 combat missions.

Two planes flew 121 missions each. Eight planes flew over 100 missions. 120 planes flew 10 missions or less.

French Maquis

On August 1, 1944, I had been scheduled to fly my 29th mission. In the early hours of the morning on the days I flew, I left my bed with mixed emotions. It was in the state of half sleep and half consciousness that I stumbled toward breakfast at the mess hall one-quarter of a mile away. I walked with others, but mostly in silence. Thoughts, thousands of thoughts, dashed through my head; and at this hour, my brain was incapable of doing anything with all of the impulses it was receiving.

What was our target to be? How far into Europe would this mission take us today? What was the weather like on the other side of the Channel? Were our fighters going to be able to help us all the way to the target and back? Flak, ya, what about the amount of flak we could expect this day? How many German fighters would be awaiting us? I only have six more missions to go so could this be the one that will have my name on it? Which crew will I be assigned to as a lead navigator? Wonder what we will have for breakfast? Questions, questions—but no answers.

When we sat down at briefing, I learned that I would be flying with the Charlie Besser Crew. I had been with them before so a certain amount of comfort settled in with this information. As the curtain was pulled back, we could see that our mission was deep into France, almost to the Swiss border. The exciting news came when the Briefing Officer stated that the mission today would be one in which we would drop supplies to the French Maquis. It was designated as Target No. 13.

These groups of brave men, women, and even children were still fighting the German war machine, long after their country had been captured and had surrendered. They hid in the mountains and countryside and continuously harassed the Germans. They blew up staff cars; they wrecked train engines; they tore up railroad tracks; they blew up bridges; they destroyed or appropriated supplies and equipment; they helped prisoners to escape, and generally they were a thorn in the German's side. Their missions were a hit and run technique. They would plan their attacks with the element of surprise on their side. They knew that being caught meant torture prior to being killed.

105

Today, my heart swelled up when I learned that I would be able to help, in a small way, this brave group of partisans. We were going to deliver canisters and barrels of supplies that would be parachuted down to our friends and allies in the midst of the Germans. These canisters contained small arms, ammunition, explosives, food, medical supplies, and whatever they requested through the underground. We all felt really close to the resistance fighters in the French underground movement.

Today, we would be going to Lac d' Anncey, France. Our drop area was high in the mountains on a plateau. The French were surrounded by their German enemy, but the price the Germans had to pay to rid themselves of this nuisance would be very high. Periodically, the Germans sent out patrols to hit the French or they would bomb suspected areas that they believed the Maquis occupied. Most of these efforts were futile, however.

The 95th Bomb Group was a part of a huge formation that the 3rd Division sent out this day. Our Group's target was a drop area near the Swiss border. We would leave England at a 20,000 ft. altitude and then gradually drop down to the deck as we approached our target. We would return to England at this low altitude, a new experience for each of us. There would be some advantages to this method of travel from our drop zone, but there would also be some disadvantages and dangers.

By flying low, we could avoid or certainly confuse German radar. At this low altitude, if we were attacked by German fighters, we would be relatively safe on the belly side of our formation, which was a favorite angle of attack by the "Jerries." Another advantage was the fact that we could see firsthand the beautiful French countryside.

The disadvantage of this low level return trip was the difficulty in navigating because landmarks raced by or were not visible and the direction of surface winds were constantly changing. If we were hit by fighters, our parachutes were of no value, since we had little chance of leaving the plane, let alone opening a chute. We were also vulnerable to small arms fire from ground operated machine guns and even rifles.

This day, the 95th Bomb Group was made up of 26 B-17s. Once we were underway, we would alter course several times in order to confuse the Germans concerning our actual intentions. On the early part of our flight, we were escorted by our "Little Brothers," which was always a good feeling. Once we crossed the German front lines, our formation started to let down. In the meantime, the mountains of France were beginning to raise up to meet us. We were only about 100 miles from the target when we spotted Mt. Blanc with its white peak, some 14,000 feet in elevation. What a thrill. Soon, I was able to spot the Matterhorn in the Swiss Alps. We knew that Target No. 13 was about 60 kilometers due East of Mt. Blanc so our problem now was to pinpoint the exact plateau near Lac d' Anncey. Our specific target would be three burning straw stacks in a clearing.

In perfect formation we dropped below the ridges of the mountains and moved just above the valley floor. We could see the red roofs of some French farm houses in the mountains. At times, it seemed that parts of these valleys were too narrow for our formation. Everything seemed to be so intimate. Our formation dropped to an altitude of 500 ft. to unload our canisters of supplies.

At a prearranged signal, several flares were fired from our lead plane and at the same time the fires were spotted from the clearing, which was dead ahead. As we flew over the drop zone, we noted that a large number of the French Partisans had lined themselves up in the form of the Cross of Lorraine. This gesture on the part of our French friends brought tears to my eyes.

So much of this terrible war seemed remote, but today I could look out of the nose of our B-17 and could feel that I could almost touch these people below me. We had never met but this was not important. We were doing something on this day that did not require imagination . If our efforts could help shorten this war by only a few days, it seemed worth the risk and the effort.

With our rendezvous spotted, the entire formation swung around, flew down another valley, zoomed up several times to avoid high hills, and then began our run to the target. After a wide arc down a twisting avenue of interlocked valleys, the formation reapproached the designated plateau and the bomb bay doors opened. Thousands of red, white, and yellow parachutes billowed out over the large field; and as the supplies floated down, hundreds of Maquis ran from hidden trucks. They waved happily, scooped up the chutes and containers, and made a beeline back to the trucks. Mission accomplished and time to head for home.

Our flight back to England was a few hundred feet above the ground. This meant that we would be dropping our altitude as we left the mountain area of France. No enemy planes had been encountered, though all eyes of our gunners were alerted to this danger. We passed over the French countryside so fast that you had little time to enjoy the beautiful landscape on a sunny day in early August. The tail gunners of each Fortress perhaps had the best seat to enjoy this spectacular view.

As the ground raced past us at nearly 150 miles per hour or about 220 feet per second, it seemed that time passed rapidly. Despite that, it took the formation nearly 2 1/2 hours to come within sight of the Channel. On the outskirts of Dunkerque, one of our gunners spotted a German Flak Tower dead ahead. All guns that could be trained forward were aimed at this unexpected target. The tower appeared to be about 100 feet high

108 • French Maquis

Picture of a monument built by the French government after the war as a tribute to these brave French partisans. The monument is built at Plateau Des Glieres, Hautesavois, France. The sculptor was Gilioi and it is titled "Monument National A La Resistance."

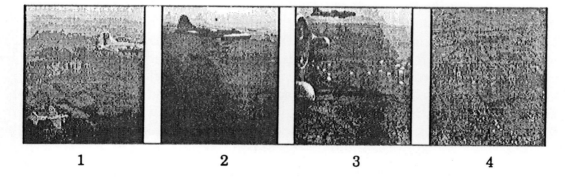

The sequence of pictures were taken with an inexpensive Browny camera of the mission to drop supplies to the French Maquis just southeast of Switzerland near Mt. Blanc, from 500 feet altitude.
    No. 1 - entering valley
    No. 2 - dropping canisters
    No. 3 - chutes open
    No. 4 - circling back over drop area

with many Germans racing around the upper deck. As thousands of 50 caliber shells converged on this rapidly approaching target, we could see dozens of Germans leaping over the railing, falling over 100 feet to the ground. We have no way of knowing how many of the enemy were killed, but the sight shall always remain with me as an added plus to this already successful mission.

If a mission can be looked upon with positive memories, this particular day will be remembered with a great deal of fondness. We lost no planes nor flyers this day, while we had accomplished so much. This type of mission turned out to be so successful that the French Maquis, with the supplies and equipment, were able to reclaim Paris even before the battleline had caught up with the city.

At the interrogation debriefing, all agreed that this mission gave them more satisfaction than any other trip that we had made. The excitement from all who had participated told the whole story.

The additional part of my participation had to wait until July of 1989 when my wife Norma had a chance to visit France, Switzerland, and Italy. By chance, her friends in Europe took her to a National Monument built at Plateau Des Glieres, Haute-Savoice, France. At this very spot where I had been in 1944, the French Government had constructed a monument to those brave Maquis titled "Monument National A La Resistance." Norma had a chance to talk to some of the people who were the recipients of our dropped canisters. Many of these Partisans had been killed or tortured, but all agreed that it was necessary to resist the German enemy. These people even used the silk from the chutes that we dropped, as well as the metal from the canisters.

All expressed their appreciation to Norma for our efforts to help them in their great cause. I wish that I had been with her to see these things at Target No. 13, with the code name "Operation Cadillac."

The Girl I Left Behind

This chapter in the story of my war years developed much the same way as the others. All of the stories started out by being awake at night and letting my mind and memories unfold. The thoughts that pass through my head during these moments developed into a chronological order in which the most minute details become real and are lived once again.

As I look up at the ceiling in the darkness with closed eyes, I see each moment unfold in their rightful sequence. I see details develop that I had almost forgotten, and I am now aware of reasons for happenings that I never knew before. Tonight, as in the past, I will get up and start writing, letting my words flow from my mind and heart, through my right arm and hand into whatever pen or pencil is handy.

This night, however, my aroused emotions have taken on a deeper feeling than when I was moved to write about a specific combat mission or some particular experience. For some unknown reason that has nothing to do with priorities, I now feel moved to record my earliest relationship with NORMA, both before and during the war.

Just as I start writing about perhaps the most important part of my life, there is some confusion as to the best way one should start in order to give real understanding for the love that grew with each day. I also am not so sure that there is anything unique about our story and relationship; however, tonight it is important to let my feelings fall into words and sentences, thus creating thoughts that have been buried for over 45 years.

Norma Ann Schmidt and I attended the same high school in Wausau, Wisconsin. She was a grade behind me and we, somehow, never had the opportunity to meet or know each another. I knew that she existed because I was aware that she had been crowned "Transportation Queen" for the city of Wausau, a celebration of note that the famous street cars were about to be retired for more modern buses. She also had been crowned "Donut Dutchess," an honor bestowed upon her by her fellow students. I had the distinction during this period of selling the most dozen donuts—for whatever the cause—thus permitting me to cast a vote

Norma Ann Schmidt
"The girl I left behind"

for each dozen. I cast all of my cherished votes for a friend who lost to Norma. She made a most impressive queen.

We met for the very first time when we both attended the University of Wisconsin at Madison. I had stayed out of school for a year to earn enough money for my education. We both were now freshmen, 150 miles from home. Norma entered school as a pre-nurse scholar, and I had enrolled in the School of Engineering. On a Saturday in October 1941, the day Wisconsin played Ohio State in football, a mutual friend, Frank Morman, brought us together for the first time. We went out on an afternoon date. I dated Norma's roommate, Nathalie Johnson, and Frank dated Norma. I knew at this first meeting that I had discovered the person that I was supposed to be looking for. As I look back, this first meeting with the four of us was frivolous and quite trivial. The importance of this chance meeting is that the spark that was to ignite my life had just appeared for the first time.

Several weeks transpired before a very shy freshman could muster the courage to call and ask Norma for a date to our Tripp Hall House Party that took place on Picnic Point on Lake Mendota. Yes, she would go. As I hung up the phone, I had my first and still memorable emotion. We were going to get to know one another. However, as a neophyte lover, I spent most of this first date talking about her cousin, a very good friend of mine. I really don't believe that I earned any "brownie points" this night. The most important thing that I accomplished was having the courage to ask her out on several other occasions.

Since both of us were students with difficult academic obligations, and the fact that both of us came from families of modest means, there were not too many occasions that we had both the time and money for dates. I do recall having a Sunday night dinner at an authentic Chinese restaurant in a secluded booth, and I remember the night of December 7, 1941, when both of us were together and walked over to the Armory to learn that two of our friends from high school had been killed.

Before the end of the school year, we seemed to drift apart. I had been in R.O.T.C. and the draft had caught up to me. I had much on my mind, and Norma felt that she did not want to be restricted by going steady. Perhaps this fateful separation had some meaning that I could not then, nor now, understand. We saw each other only a single time, quite by accident, on a bus ride from Madison to Wausau. At this moment, it appeared that our paths and lives were not destined to cross again.

In July 1942, my mother, who knew and liked Norma, somehow in her crafty way, conned her into visiting our home. When I accidently entered the house and discovered Norma sitting in my living room, I immediately realized that the original spark had not gone out but only flickered. I had just enlisted in the United States Air Force as a cadet and she was about to go into nurse's training at Rochester, Minnesota. We both agreed to keep in contact with one another via the mails. Neither of us knew at the time where this relationship was heading nor that our entire courtship would be conducted by letters.

On January 17, 1943, I left for Nashville, Tennessee, and the beginning of my cadet training. I would not return home and see Norma again until January, 1944. At that time, I had completed my military training and had been commissioned a Second Lieutenant in the Air Force as a navigator. I also had received my orders to report for combat after a month leave of absence. Norma managed to get a two-day pass from school in Chicago and arrived home on the 22nd. At 2 A.M. on the 23rd of January, 1944, I proposed to her, she accepted, and we became engaged. It was an understood fact that the size and quality of the diamond that I gave her this cool crisp morning was not a true measurement of my feelings. From this moment, my inner thoughts would never be the same.

In England with the 95th Bomb Group flying B17s, I became very involved in my contributions in the war. After my ninth mission over Germany, I was made a lead navigator, a position that required a great deal of my concentration, but one that would get me through my tour of duty months ahead of the other members of my crew. I wrote Norma many times each week in a faithful manner and received letters from her with the same regularity. I have had the opportunity to re-read these letters many times over the ensuing years, and I now realize that they contained only partial feelings. Because of the censorship during the war, I could not write too much about my flying and those experiences during combat missions. On my days off when I escaped to London or some other interesting place, the fact that I could not share them with her made these moments less important. I did write in general terms about these trips and I did express my love and how I missed her. I now know that my deep feeling came when I was alone in my thoughts, whether in my bunk or on a lonely walk, not when I sat down to write home.

On many nights, I left the base and walked by myself along a narrow English road at a slow pace. Perhaps I would flop on a grassy bank against a hedgerow and stare up into the clear night sky, knowing I would see the same stars that stood over Rochester. I would listen to the night songs of the nightingale and would have given anything to have Norma beside me at this special moment. Some of my most difficult moments came when the German radio station with Axis Sally or Lord HaHa would play the French Song, "Lilly Marlene." God their propaganda took its toll during these brief moments. These were the times that I thought of Norma and my heart ached to be with her.

I knew that it was only the flip of a coin as to whether I would be one of the lucky ones to finish my tour of 35 combat missions. It was a fact that half of the crews did not make it and there was no way I could alter these odds. My religious beliefs did not permit me to pray or beg that I should be the lucky one to make it through this war. I only survived on the hope that this lad from Wausau might make it home in one piece and have the opportunity to spent the rest of his life with the girl he had chosen to be his wife. This hope is the one thing that kept me motivated.

My relationship with my parents was never close and endearing. The emotional inspiration I received from the letters I got from Norma helped me endure the constant pressures only mortal combat can place upon you. I look back now, nearly 47 years later, and I realize that our entire courtship was done through these hundreds of letters that crossed the Atlantic in both directions.

We had practically no true memories that a long lasting relationship would bring because there was little personal contact before our long separation. The number of embraces, the kisses, and the moments together could be counted on one's fingers. How do you relive these brief moments in time through the mails, especially letters you knew would be censored by strange and uncaring eyes? Yes, today I could recount millions of moments that we've had together, each very special and important to me. From England I could only express my love and what she meant to me in a somewhat diluted way, not by choice, but because of all of the extenuating circumstances.

I tried to hide the uncertainty of my coming back in one piece and also to conceal my deepest fears of combat and the war. I realize now that I had built a callus and invisible wall around myself, and especially around my feelings in order to get through each day and night and to keep my sanity. The only times I seemed to crack this wall were for brief moments when I could sneak away into my own thoughts and let my real feelings escape. It was not something that I could turn on and off at will.

Looking back, I now know that I was a product of a home that did not generate much in the way of love. Seldom did I observe an embrace or even a small hug among the members of my family. There was, however, a feeling of unspoken and undisplayed affection for one another. It seemed to be important that you just don't show it. The feeling of hate or dissension was as absent as the emotions of love. Four kids were raised in the atmosphere of a strict German household. I had to learn, from square one, the meaning of the emotion love and the feelings that grow when one gets involved.

These deep and new feelings were explored and developed during my quite moments when I would be in my own thoughts. My closest friend in combat was Dan Waddell from Hendersonville, North Carolina, who got married only a few days before we took off for England. On rare occasions we would talk about serious matters, but usually his friendship was most valuable for its lighter moments. At different times, my mind tried to explore the future, and I wondered if Norma and I would be truly compatible. Would she enjoy nature as I did? Would she understand my compassion for being active in most sports? Would I recognize her needs and ambitions? Were we truly meant for each other so that we could both grow, or somehow would we tend to stunt one another? These, and many other thoughts, hopes, desires, and wishes flashed through my mind.

During these many months apart, I discovered that, although I did not really enjoy poetry, I did appreciate certain poems. When I discovered a poetic endeavor that expressed some of my feelings, feelings that were difficult to put into my own words when I wrote to Norma, I would then copy and send her a particular poem. A typical example of one of these many poems is the following (perhaps my very favorite):

WAIT FOR ME

Wait for me—I will come back.
only wait. . . . and wait.
Wait though rain clouds glowering black make you desolate;
Wait though winter snowstorms whirl,
Wait though summer's hot
Wait though no one else will wait and past forgot;
Wait though from the distant front, not one letter comes;
Wait though everyone who waits sick of it becomes.
Wait for me . . . . I will come back.
Pay no heed to those who'll so glibly tell you that it is vain to wait.
Though my mother and my son think that I am gone,
Though my friends abandon hope
And back there at home rise and toast my memory, wrapped in silence pained,
Wait. And when they drink that toast leave your glass undrained.
Though from Death's own jaws
Let the friends who did not wait
Think it chance, no more.
They will never understand
Those who did not wait
How we, your waiting that saved me in the war.
And the reason I've come though we shall know, we two;
Simply this, you waited as
No one else could do.

by Konstantin Simonor, (Russian)

As I look back to these early days of the war, I now know that the strict and almost regimented way that I had been brought up was more conducive to withstand the exposure to war than to be a romantic or caring person. Somehow, though, all through all of this ordeal, I did develop sensitivity about things in nature and particularly about people.

On September 13, 1944, I left England and combat for home and boarded the Queen Mary. It took until October 13th to reach Wausau and Norma. Early in the morning after the train pulled into the depot in Rothschilds, the porter fell out of the train while carrying my heavy B-4 bag and my even heavier duffel bag. As I was bending over to help him and watching Norma run along the platform with outstretched arms, I could see the noses of literally hundreds of passengers pressed against the glass, watching two lovers meet after a long, long separation. This vivid and memorable scene will remain with me always. It was obvious that the Porter had passed the news of the reunion down the entire length of the train.

It was the day before the date scheduled for our wedding, which had to be moved back exactly one week. One of the prerequisites for getting married in the State of Wisconsin is the law that all blood tests be sent to Madison, the state capitol. Out of town guests had to be notified, etc., etc. These problems were of no concern to me. I was home with my Norma Ann.

On Saturday at 4 P.M., we were united in marriage in a rather large church wedding. The reception, the dinner, and the dance continued into the wee hours of the following Sunday. Several unique things about our wedding shall always be remembered by the two of us. Namely, I was one of the first to return to Wausau from combat so many citizens of the town became involved. I was married in my officer's uniform. Norma's father, her uncle and brother-in-law and my father had worked for weeks fixing and repainting an old Ford Model A car. They transported Norma and me through the uptown area after the wedding ceremony. It was a one car parade during the 5 o'clock rush. Finally, the dance brought together relatives who had not spoken to one another in years. The atmosphere and the prevailing mood made this evening have a therapeutic affect on all who attended.

After a brief honeymoon in northern Wisconsin, Norma had to return to Minnesota and school. I was sent to a rest and relaxation facility at Miami Beach, Florida; a facility that had been set up for returning airmen. The separation from my new bride was most difficult, especially having to go to the beaches of sunny Florida by myself. My temperament and training made me realize that this was yet another sacrifice that one makes during a war. The several weeks we had together now gave me memories that I did not have while in combat. My R & R in the southeast was nice, but it was not nice.

To my amazement, shortly after January 1945, when I traveled up to Rochester, Minnesota, to visit Mrs. Krueger, I was informed that she

118 • The Girl I Left Behind

Wedding Day - October 21, 1944

had done a considerable amount of soul searching and had come to the conclusion that she would leave nurses training and become a full-time wife and partner by being with me while I finished my military obligation. Though her mother and immediate family believed that I had influenced this decision, nothing could have been further from the truth. I did not regret then that Norma chose to come with her mate, nor do I have doubts today that those moments together were ill spent. No one can tell for sure that the paths each of us choose to walk down are not the right ones—just as we can not know the consequences should we decide to take a different route.

On January 10, 1945, Norma and I left for Ellington Field near Houston, Texas. The next day we got a ride to Texas City and found our first little house to rent. We had complete privacy and the proverbial bliss one reads about. We now had a pad from which we could grow together. My orders to report to Ellington Field were for the further training required and to determine where my services as a trained navigator were going to be needed for our continuing war effort. I chose the Air Transport Command, the A.T.C.

On March 13, 1945, Norma and I were sent to St. Joseph, Missouri, at Rosecrans Field, where my duties required that I ferry new aircraft to various parts of the world and on occasions, return war weary planes to the U.S.A. My work required that I travel to a remote place approximately every two weeks. During this time, I would be assured of at least three days free from duty and time to spend with my wife. By ingenuity and a few other tricks, I managed to average over a week together between trips. My only real problem on the flights to distant lands was that I could not share these experiences with Norma. I saw so many strange sights and different cultures in South America, Africa, Europe, The Caribbean Islands, throughout the Pacific Ocean and every corner of the United States. The edge came off from each of these experiences because I felt that we now had four eyes and two minds. Only half of our faculties would be present. I kept dreaming of ways to sneak her along on these assignments; and if it had not been impossible to get her back into the country through customs, I believe it would have been possible.

Norma and I lived in our second floor apartment near the center of St. Joseph, Missouri, until October, when she traveled back to Wausau and I went to Sioux Falls, South Dakota, to receive my discharge and separation from the U.S. Air Force. The war was nearly over and it was our turn to take charge of our own destiny. On October 24, 1945, I headed for Wausau. I was a civilian; I was out of a job, and in three months I'd become a father. After combat, all of these outlooks did little to deter my excitement about getting home to truly start our life with my partner and friend. My plans were to continue my education in the Architecture School at the University of Michigan.

The four years that had transpired from the moment that I had first met Norma, until we finally had control of our destiny, seemed both short and also an eternity. These were the growing years for my feelings and emotions. I had to learn the most fundamental expressions for how I felt—how to verbally say, "I love you"; how to hold hands in public; how to give a kiss at any moment if I felt like it; and how to just let Norma and any glancing eye know that we cared for each other. It was important that we let our feelings show. Though it was a slow and often difficult process, steady emotional growth did occur. Today, 47 years later, we do not take a backseat to anyone.

Mission No. 30— "A Milk Run"

In the early hours of the morning of August 2, 1944, the usual wake up call was taking place for the crew members scheduled for the mission of the day. This morning, for some reason, was different for me. On most mission days, I found that my internal clock would awaken me and get me going. On this peaceful morning, however, I needed the gentle tap and whisper to remind me that it was time to rise and shine. Instead of spending a restless night and hours of thinking about what might occur and what fate the next flight might bring, I had slept like a baby and would not see the enlisted man from Personnel enter the darkened barracks with his flashlight and check each bed in order to find those crew members who would get the opportunity to visit some place in Europe once again. This night's sleep had prepared me for what was to come.

Several of us in our barracks got dressed and stumbled out into the dark, damp, early morning English air and made our way to the mess hall. Most conversations were conducted with grunts and groans. Being alert was a foreign word at this ungodly hour. In the dimly lit mess hall, many cigarettes had already been ignited and layers of thin smoke floated over the long tables at which sat the groggy airmen. On the days that we flew, we were offered all of the fresh eggs that we desired. This does not sound like a big deal unless you've had the opportunity to taste the eggs that would be served later to the crews left behind. Instead of telling the cook that you would like you eggs over easy, you would be given scrambled eggs that had a definite green hue. These were known as the infamous powdered eggs of World War II. I might add that they tasted worse than they looked.

At the briefing for the mission, I learned many positive things that began to make this day seem special. First, our mission was a Tactical Target, a bridge just east of Paris, France. This would be considered a short flight over Europe, one that would count as another mission, my thirtieth. Second, we were told that the weather would be perfect. The sky would be free of clouds and the complete flight would have more than adequate friendly air protection by our fighters. Third, our scheduled flight pattern to the target area would take us largely over the area that our ground forces had liberated in France. It had been almost two months since D-Day, so our troops had pushed well south of the invasion coast and had created a large bulge in western France. Flying over occupied territory meant that we would only be exposed to flak in the target area. Fourth, and perhaps the best sign that this would be an easy credit for a mission, was the knowledge that our crew was scheduled to have a General from Headquarters fly with us as an observer. He did not have flight status and this would be his first experience on a mission that would enable him to witness the life of a typical bomber crew. The fact that he was present and would be flying with us meant that my 30th mission was going to be a "milk run." Was I wrong.

At the briefing we were told that the bridge to be knocked out was important to the advancing troops and that we should not expect flak nor enemy fighters until we reached the target area. We'd cross the Channel on the south side of England and enter France just East of Caen, a place I remember well because I had previously visited this exact spot on June 6th, D-Day. The Allied Forces had now pushed south and east and possessed much of the territory that we were to fly over on our way to Paris.

This morning, with the sun now rising, with the sleep well out of our eyes, and with the General aboard, we were all in high spirits. A great deal of joking was going on between the gunners, as we each assumed our stations in the B-17. We were a lead crew so each of the members had a great deal of experience, and we were accustomed to getting ourselves into the routine of doing our respective jobs. On this day, however, we wouldn't be flying in the lead position of the 95th Bomb Group; we'd be taking the number two spot in the lead squadron. This meant we would fly to the left, slightly below and a short distance back of Lt. R. O. Baber and his crew.

The take-off, the rendezvous over Buncher 8, our trip to Splasher 7 after the Group had assembled, and the flight in formation toward the south coast of England went without incident. Because the weather was clear, our Pathfinder plane left our formation and headed toward the 100th Bomb Group and a different target deeper into France. At this point we still had 32 planes in our formation.

As we approached the coast south of London, Lt. Curley's plane, number 231600, aborted because of failure of his number 2 engine and turned back. Shortly thereafter, Lt. A.P. Salvia's plane had a failure in his number 2 engine, and he peeled off to return to base. Now we were down to 30 Fortresses from the 95th.

Shortly after we entered France and were passing over the frontlines below, holy hell suddenly broke loose. Without any warning, we ran into a large group of flak bursts. We learned later that a crack German artillery unit had raised their 88mm guns skyward and had guessed our altitude and range accurately. Instantly, the beautiful blue sky turned both black and threatening. At the same moment that we could feel a direct hit on our plane, we could also see that Lt. Baber's lead ship had started to blow up as he veered below us. As plane number 2102700 went by us, it was a ball of fire. The red and yellow flames against the black smoke of the flak was indescribable. I could feel the intense heat on my face as I watched the plane break apart. Pieces were flying in all directions from their plane, as we also fell away from the Group.

Somehow three crew members managed to leave Lt. Baber's plane and get their chutes open. These were busy moments for us, as we tried to determine our own damage while being concerned about the fate of our lead plane. We knew that we were going down, yet we knew that the men in Baber's ship were in greater danger. Seconds seemed like minutes. My right window had been broken by exploding debris so it was very difficult to see if chutes were leaving the other plane. In these first moments, there was more concern for the Baber crew than our own fate.

The three men who were lucky enough to escape this flaming wreckage were D.W. Phillips, the ball turret gunner; B. Lipkin, waist gunner; and W.J. Collyer, tail gunner. All would be taken captives by the Germans and spend the remainder of the war as P.O.Ws. Killed in action were: Lt. R.O. Baber, pilot; J.W. Kalor, co-pilot; R.D. Dallas, navigator; F.T. Sohm, bombardier; O.C. Warod, top turret gunner; R.V. Hill, radio operator; and E.E. Bockman, observer.

The hit that took us out of formation was under our right wing, and it immediately knocked out our numbers 3 and 4 engines. The pilot or co-pilot quickly tried to feather these two props. Number four engine propellor responded and the three blades gradually turned into the wind and became frozen into a fixed position. The number 3 engine's propellors did not respond and kept windmilling as we lost altitude. Pieces of the cowling and parts of the housing were breaking off and hitting the plane.

During all of this confusion, we had the problem of the General who had come along as an observer, much to his dismay. He had been standing behind the seats of the pilots when the sudden burst of flak was thrown up at our formation. I'm sure that he was as surprised as the rest of us. He immediately came down to the area between my navigational compartment and the escape hatch on the floor. The General was six foot tall and had a good build, and I had noticed that he had snapped his parachute onto his chest harness, which made him look even larger. As he moved into the nose area, it was apparent that there was not room for the bombardier, myself, and this large person. This was the one and only time in my military career that I told a General to haul his butt out of here and go to the waist position of the plane. On a mission or anytime an airplane is airborne, the navigator is able to use his rank, when the safety of the airplane and crew are concerned.

The General turned to go back into the waist of the plane where there was slightly more room. He immediately got himself hung up as he was crossing the cat walk in the bomb bay. His parachute harness got hooked onto some of the shackles that protruded and it appeared he could not free himself. I heard what I thought was a loud yell and could just barely see his problem. This was all taking place as the plane was sliding downward and the noise level was tremendous. I got on the intercom and asked the top turret gunner, our engineer, to help free the General. By the time he came down, the radio operator had the "Big Boy" through the bomb bay and into his radio compartment, which was void of windows and free of the mayhem taking place around us. I'm sure that this nervous General was happy to only hear and feel the commotion and not witness our predicament.

We had lost a fair amount of altitude before the plane was brought under control. The pilot had the difficult task of flying our B-17 with only two left engines. With our only power in an unsymmetrical condition, it took skill and control to get this falling plane into a level flight position. The first turn of our plane was in a northwest direction to get over friendly territory. Pieces of the engine housing kept flying off into the plane with such force as to cut and dent the aluminum skin.

My primary job was to determine our exact position and give the pilot a heading that could take us home. The quickest method to determine our immediate location was with the British Gee Box, an instrument that was normally useless over occupied Europe because the Germans would jam it. Today, we were in luck, mostly because we still were fairly close to England and the source of the signals. As I bent down to work the equipment, it was necessary for me to turn my back to the windmilling propeller and the chunks of metal being thrown into the plane. A few weeks prior to this eventful day, I had seen a picture in the Stars & Stripes, our service newspaper, of a similar plane with a runaway prop. It had ultimately flown off, had one blade enter the nose of the plane, and had killed the navigator. This was all that I could think of as I knelt down and made calculations from my British Gee Box. Sweat was running down my spine as I finally got the information that I needed to give the pilot a heading for home.

I gave the pilot a heading that would take us over friendly territory held by the Allies and that would provide the least amount of Channel water to cross. We were going to head for the tip of Cherbourg. We wanted to spent most of our flight over land, should bailing out become necessary.

In the meantime, it was decided to dump our four 1000# bombs to lighten the plane and to maintain altitude. Normally, when we had targets in France, Belgium, or the Netherlands, the bombs would be brought back if the target area was obscured or if conditions were such that we could not be sure of the results. Civilians in occupied countries would not be killed unnecessarily. Today, our safety required that these bombs leave the airplane. We did not want to land with only two engines and these bombs. We also were not sure at this point how badly damaged our landing gear might be.

The bombardier was instructed to pick a clear area and drop all 4,000 pounds of our bombs. When he released our load after opening the bomb bay doors, only one bomb dropped. We knew immediately that the other three were hung up by the reaction of the plane. Normally when the bombs are released, the plane jumps upward, relieved of the additional load. The single bomb dropping away from the plane hardly improved the attitude of the B-17. The bombardier discovered that he was unable to toggle any of the remaining three bombs free of their shackles. Knowing what needed to be done, the engineer left his post and took a screw driver with him into the bomb bay. With some effort he was able to free each of the bombs individually. The first two bombs appeared to hit in open areas but the third missile landed near a French farmyard, causing a great deal of damage.

About this time we were aware that we had attracted a group of four P-47s. Flying over Allied territory with a lone B-17 with its bomb doors open and dropping individual bombs on targets below attracted more than curiosity from these four friendly fighter planes. It was common knowledge that the Germans had several of our B-17s and would often fly close to our formations in order to send back information to the German fighters or flak guns. We were lucky because we were a lead plane and were able to monitor our own fighters and explain the situation. They escorted us to the tip of Cherbourg; a big brother and his four little friends.

Once we crossed the Channel, I left my position at the navigator's table and did dead reckoning from a position behind the two pilots. We all were very apprehensive about the windmilling prop, which was getting worse by the minute. Each of us knew that if the propeller flew off, it could go in any direction. Slowly, we made our way back to Horham, England, the base of the 95th Bomb Group. Even though we did not get a chance to drop our bomb load on the target near Paris, the remaining 28 B-17s from our Group arrived back at the field before us. The last of the planes were landing as we approached the field. Our control tower was aware of our problems and precautions were taken if we had to crash land.

126 • Mission No. 30—"A Milk Run"

Awards Ceremony, Headquarters Building, Horham. (USAF)

August 4, 1944—This is a photograph of First Lieutenant Lloyd O. Krueger receiving the distinquished flying cross, the highest award that the U.S. Air Force bestows.

Just as we touched down with our underpowered airplane, the jar was enough to make the number three propeller drop off unto the runway. We were again very lucky when this three-bladed prop flew to the right so that the tire on that side of the plane did not have to run over it. This obstacle could have caused our plane to ground loop or crack up. The squeaking of the brakes and the slowing of our forward motion were welcomed sounds and certainly a grateful feeling of relief.

Everyone left the plane with extreme gratitude, which was a feeling I learned to appreciate on many of my previous missions. The right side of the plane was a mess, with two engines out, lots of wing damage, and the right forward skin scarred and torn up from both flak and metal from the engine housing. As I left the plane, I had completely forgotten about our General passenger. When he exited from the rear door and had his feet on the pavement at the hardstand, he made it a point to shake each crew member's hand. He apologized to the officers for any problems that he might have caused and he informed all who would listen that he had flown his first and last mission. Unfortunately, this also was the last mission for Lt. Baber and his entire crew.

 BLITZ OVER POLITZ

Thursday night and my butt was really dragging. Today, August 24, 1944, I flew my 31st mission to Ruhland, Germany, to hit another synthetic oil refinery. This turned out to be a long haul, deep into Germany, and we were hit several times by enemy fighters. The flak over the target was more intense than usual. These days, it became an expected greeting when we flew over the "fatherland." I had flown lead navigator with Lt. M.J. Giles and crew.

On this particular mission, at 1253 hours, just as we were unloading our bombs, Lt. D.J. Schmidt radioed that he had been hit; that his no. 2 engine was knocked out, that he was losing altitude, and that he could not keep up. He dropped back and joined another B-17 in trouble. At 1350 hours Lt. Schmidt radioed that that he had just lost no. 4 engine and they were losing valuable altitude. The crew bailed out at coordinates 51°50'N and 9° 30'E, somewhere near Gottingen, Germany. The co-pilot was Lt. E.E. Paulson, the navigator was Lt. E.M. Jenkins, and the bombardier was Lt. H. L. Eustice. The gunners were Sargeants Watson, Hyatt, McQuade, Ward, and Kelly. All of these crew members ended up being P.O.W.s.

On this warm Thursday night, I walked over to the Officer's Club really bushed. I knew from experience that a few drinks would relax me and put more spring into my walk. The bar tonight would close at 2000 hr because an alert flag had been raised at Squadron Headquarters, indicating that tomorrow's weather should be conducive for another raid somewhere in Germany. My plans for just flaking out on Friday were suddenly changed when I found my name on the schedule to fly lead again with Lt. Charlie Lajeskie and his crew. This news gave me mixed emotions. First, I was happy to get a chance to get my 32nd mission in and approach a little closer to the magic number 35 and my return to the States. On the downside, the few drinks I had consumed didn't erase the memories that I had floating through my head of the mission I had just returned from a few hours ago. It seemed that just moments ago that I had just left "Lady Fortune," No. 297858 and the Lt. Gilles crew, thankful for being back at Horham and the 95th Base and looking forward to a day or two to recharge my batteries.

My walk back to my barracks was slow and in silence. Even the melodic singing of the ever present nightingale along my path could not seem to drown out some of the thoughts racing through my tired head. The paramount doubt that kept chewing away at me was wondering how long my luck would continue. Would I be able to fly four more missions and still come back to hear the varied songs of this British nightingale, a very special member of the thrush family. I had been flying long enough, though, to know that it was not too healthy to dwell on these thoughts. Some of my friends who couldn't escape these strong inner fears and emotions were the ones who broke and were sent home. I did not want to return for that reason, but my hope for some of these friends was that time would completely erase their personal negative experiences.

The 0300 hour wake-up call came long before I was ready; the breakfast was as tasteless as yesterday; my nervous cigarette seemed unusually unnecessary; and on this morning, most of the guys walking toward the Briefing Room preferred the silence of their own thoughts.

It didn't take long to find out the target. We were going to Politz, Germany, a small city on Lake Mritz in the northeast corner of this hostile country, near the Baltic Sea. We were told to expect German fighters and that the flak would be the quantity and quality of most well-defended German targets. We got the usual statement: "Gentlemen, this is the type of target you do not want to return to get your bombs on our objective. Good luck." The only comment I uttered, almost under my breath, was—"So what's new."

We lumbered down runway 25 in a westerly direction, followed by 31 other B-17s, at 30 second intervals. We all headed northeast to Buncher 8. There was a thick cloud cover that towered above the area at a depth of over 6000 feet that each plane had to fly blind through. One by one, we broke into the sunshine and started to develop our formation. Each plane, in a prescribed order, moved behind and to one side of the lead plane and in the squadron assigned. Flying in the lead ship, I could feel the other planes gradually inch their way into position in the formation as our tail gunner kept us advised. The high squadron was now developing off to our right, while the low squadron on the left still awaited several planes to close the distance and get into position. Just about this time, we got a call from Lt. J. H. Baumgardner in 2106993 that their plane had an oxygen leak and would return to base. Shortly thereafter, Lt. Braund in 338067 "Joyride," informed us that his No. 2 supercharger had failed and that he would also return to base.

By the time we reached Splasher 7 and an altitude of 26,000 feet, we became aware that three of our planes were missing. Lt. Morring, Lt.

Hendrickson, and Lt. Ellsworth each found it impossible to locate the formation and to join our ranks. This was not an unusual situation when you had to climb through a thick layer of clouds. Sometimes when a plane broke out after circling through the clouds, they would spot B-17s from other Groups off in the distance and mistakenly follow, only to find out too late that they had screwed-up. Now, it would be impossible to catch up and take part in today's mission. We were now down to 27 planes and we had to do some jockeying to rearrange the planes in order to balance each of the three squadrons. This is not as simple as it may sound.

It was 0842 hours as we left the east coast of England and headed northeast over the North Sea. The only thing visible below was the soft grey blanket of clouds. The formation was on a course that appeared to be taking us right into the beautiful rising sun. The Group, some twelve miles ahead of us, reflected these sun rays and looked like bouncing sparklers in a blue sky. The pleasant, friendly rays penetrated our plexiglass windows; and for a moment, it was difficult to think about what was ahead.

At 1050 hours we spotted the usual flak being thrown up from the Island of Helgeland. We intentionally flew a course that would keep us a safe distance away from this island off the Danish-German coast. Our fighter escort gave us somewhat of a secure feeling as we approached the north coast of Germany in the Schleswig-Holstein area. However, we didn't have long to wait before the first of the German fighters hit us. Several dozen FW190s and ME109s came out of the sun to make a single pass at us. Before they could cause too much havoc, they were engaged by our fighter escort, as the formation kept on moving on an easterly course at about 150 mph. Long before we reached our I. P. Point and the target, we could see the flak that the 390th Bomb Group was receiving. The sky over Politz was covered with ominous black clouds caused by the bursting flak shells. Our turn would be next.

As we made our run to the target, we could see several B-17s from the 390th going down. They had been hit by this wall of exploding 88mm and 105mm shells that covered the depth between the high and the low squadrons—they had our altitude determined accurately. Just as soon as we flew into this black cloud of flak, at 1304 hours, Lt. Powell radioed their 3 and 4 engines had been knocked out and their props feathered. They slowly dropped down and away as they left the formation. Hell was popping all around us. At 1305 hours, Lt. Bussen in "Mirandy" had their 3 and 4 engines on fire, but the plane left the formation under control. A minute later, at 1306 hours, "Belle In The Keyhole," piloted by Lt. Shepherd, took a direct flak burst on one wing and peeled off to the right under control.

Bombs away—B-17 explodes—none will leave this plane as it falls to earth.

Direct hit by flak.

Photographs by USAF

B-17 is hit and falling away from formation—we watch for parachutes.

As the target approached, we first dropped our smoke bomb, quickly followed by the eight 500 pound bombs from our bomb bay. The entire group released their loads as soon as they saw the smoke bomb. There did not appear to be a clear piece of the sky around us that did not have evidence of bursting flak shells. It was so dark that you could see the flashes at the instant that the shells exploded. This truly was German blitz over Politz. The word "blitz" in German means lightning.

Just as our bomb bay doors closed, we could see Lt. Peery in "Hamawa" take a direct hit. Their no. 3 engine was on fire, and we could see him put the plane in a steep dive to try to extinguish the flames. As he leveled out below us, our gunners counted nine parachutes leaving the B-17. Shortly, thereafter, the plane exploded as it hit the ground. Lt. Peery, co-pilot Daniels, navigator Kieinman, bombardier Merlo, and the gunners Maffetone, Sulick, Delvellar, Nat, and Sutphin would all be captured and remain behind as P.O.W.s.

At 1330 hours we got word from our fighters that Lt. Bussen and his crew had bailed out over Sweden and would be interned for the duration of the war. Their plane exploded at coordinates 54°25' N and 12°58'E. About the same time, we found out that Lt. Powell in 46085 had their crew bail over Germany. Gunners O. E. Covel, H. Schneider, and B.E. Brileg had been killed; all others were P.O.W.s. We found out later that Lt. Shepherd and his entire crew were taken prisoners by the Germans.

Out of the original 32 planes that took off from our Base at Horham, we were now down to 23 B-17s that were limping home in a tight but smaller formation. Nearly every plane had at least one feathered prop and there were many visible signs of battle damage. After we landed we were told that 14 of our planes received notable battle scars.

Two of the crew members in our plane were slightly wounded, but many of the other planes had some seriously wounded men. I again collected several pieces of spent flak from around me that I could add to my now growing collection. Through the broken clouds below us, we could again see the North Sea. So much had happened in those condensed moments since we flew over this same spot on the earth. The sun had circled around and was still in our eyes as we flew toward England. These same friendly sun rays helped to make us appreciate and to be grateful that we were heading for home.

Our lead plane was the first over the field at Horham but would be one of the last to land. Many of the planes fired off two flares, signalling that they had severely wounded men aboard or that the condition of the plane was critical. Ambulances, crash trucks, and fire engines lined the runway. Our Group, the 95th B.G., had lost nine of its planes and nearly 100 crew members in the past nine days. Despite these losses, we were still one of the luckier groups, especially in our 13 Combat Wing.

I did not know, as I walked back to my barracks, that tomorrow, Saturday, August 26th, I would be flying my third mission in as many days. Fortunately, my number 33 mission would take me to Brest, France. It would prove to be a relatively easy mission, but one which I had a strong feeling I deserved. Also this night, I had no way of knowing that in just eleven days that I would have flown my 35th mission and would be going home.

Now when I look back on these momentous days, I truly believe that each of us had been turned into individuals that were more machine than human. Somehow, each, in our own way, found a method to overcome a fear that penetrated our every fibre and were still able to function as a disciplined team. Our adversary was equally qualified to stand before us. Each day, fate would determine the results each side set out to accomplish. What a way to resolve differences of opinions.

 Fear—Not Just Another Emotion

My story, concerning the part I played during WWII, would not be complete if the subject of "Fear" was not analyzed. As I look back and relive these moments, I have a very vivid recollection of fear, which is an elusive and difficult emotion to describe.

My *Webster Collegiate Dictionary* gives a definition that alludes to the many forms and degrees that this simple four letter word can conjure. *Webster* states that "Fear" is a painful emotion marked by alarm, dread, disquiet and also an instance of this feeling. The synonyms for fear are listed as "dread," "fright," "alarm," "dismay," "consternation," "panic," "terror," and "horror."

Fear is the general term for this emotion. It intensifies as one progresses through the above synonyms. Dread emphasizes apprehension or anxiety, while fright implies the shock of sudden, startling and commonly short-lived fear. Alarm suggests the surprise and agitation excited by emminent or unexpected danger, while dismay implies deprivation of spirit, courage, or initiative. Terror would suggest the extremity of consternation while horror adds the implication of shuttering abhorrence or aversion.

From this complex definition, it is an obvious emotion, yet it almost defies an exact description because of the many degrees that a single person can experience. I have witnessed, in myself and various crew members, nearly all of the stages of fear brought on by the dangers of combat flying and the exposure to the enemy.

Like so many other events that took place during this period of history, I can only relate my recollections of personal feelings and sensations as I was exposed to German fighter pilots and often devastating flak. As I look back now, I realize that, for some unexplained reason, I apparently had the ability to overcome the many degrees of fear that seemed to excite my emotions. I'm not alluding to the usual exposure to early fear such as being called upon in class as a student, or the very first date with a girl. We all seem to take these experiences in stride and move on. The fear that is implied by this chapter could best be described as intense.

Sports and athletics taught me how to face the unknowing and eminent dangers that were ever present when one had to collide with opponents on the field of play. If you were required to throw a block or tackle at an individual on the football field and your opponent outweighed you by 50 plus pounds, then this is the moment when you put fear on the back burner. For dozens of years in baseball, I caught behind the plate and batter without the aid of a face mask. This was despite the fact that each season I received numerous shiners or black eyes; and on occasion, I was physically knocked unconscious by a foul ball or swinging bat. As I write this now, many years later, I can see how this could be interpreted as being stupid. Despite this conclusion, it did take a certain amount of courage to immediately squat behind the batter for the next pitch. In my growing years, there were many other situations where I seemed to voluntarily force myself into the need of finding ways to overcome fear.

Once I enlisted in the Air Force, I began to experience a crescendo of fear. As a cadet in flight training, I had to immediately face up to the first hurdle—the fear of flying. I entered the Air Force with no real knowledge of flying. In fact, I almost felt like I had web feet that wanted to grip the ground. Yet, to this day one of the most memorable, pleasant experiences that I can recall is the day I flew solo in a plane over Texas. I now know that the word "thrill" is in direct proportion to the "fear" that was connected to the action.

Early in 1944 I received my commission as an officer and was assigned as a navigator to a B-17 Flying Fortress crew. This exposed me to new fears that had to be mastered. At this time, my primary concerns were to instill confidence in each member of the crew, with my abilities to safely navigate our plane. One of my first duties was to navigate our B-17 plane to England, over vast stretches of arctic wilderness and thousands of miles of the Atlantic Ocean. In the ensuing months, just being part of a crew that was required to make hundreds of landings and take-offs and to fly thousands of hours exposed each of us to dangers and risks. Then there was actual combat.

Each mission required planes loaded with gasoline and bombs to take-off at 30-second intervals on a runway that always appeared to be too short. Next, we usually had to climb through a cover of clouds several thousand feet thick and fly blind on a prescribed course until we broke out into the clear. Mid-air collisions were a common occurrence while in this cloud cover. Two aircraft would fall to the earth as one, taking with them the 20 men who probably never knew what had happened. This, too, ultimately got to be routine.

The German Air Force, "Luftwaffe," had perfected many techniques to attack our formation in order to render our many planes ineffective. They threw large numbers of fighters at us, such as the FW 190s, the ME 109s, and the ME 110s. Most fighters tried to hit us from the front because of the fast rate of closure; but during an air battle, you could expect to see planes approach from any direction, whether level, high, or low. They constantly searched for weakness in our formation. Once they caused a crippled plane to leave its position, they directed a maximum effort to finish off the kill. During some battles the Germans would use ME 110s, ME 410s, HE 111s and have them fly just beyond the range of our 50 calibre machine guns. From this position, they would fire rockets into our midst. Only our friendly fighters could help us against this technique.

Once we reached the target area, we could expect "flak." This is a simple four-letter word such as "fear," and I do believe that they could be considered synonymous. The word itself comes from the German word "fliegerabwehrkanonen." Flieger, which means flyer, plus abwehr, which means defense, plus kanonen which means cannons. This cannon defense against flyers was abbreviated to the four letters F. L. A. K.

The greater the importance of the target, the more severe the amount of flak we could expect. This flak was the most dreaded because there was no alternative but to fly into and through it in order to drop our load of bombs on a target. There was no way that we could retaliate against German antiaircraft gunners. As the war progressed, the effectiveness of the Luftwaffe decreased, but the damaged caused by flak intensified and became more devastating on each successive bombing mission. The radar and other technologies improved constantly for these German guns and their crew improved their abilities with the daily practice they received.

Nearly all of my moments of consequential fear took place during my first seven or eight missions. Fighter plane attacks created a fear that I found the easiest to conquer, partially because each member of the crew could fight back. The thing that helped me the most was my feeling that my German opponent had to have courage in order to fly into the fire from our numerous B-17s and that I challenged myself to have equal bravery to face what he was attempting to do. This phase of combat was easy to relate to the days of football or hockey.

When I saw one or more of our bombers get hit and fall to earth or when I witnessed a German fighter plane explode, I would whisper a few choice words of profanity under my breath and try to get busier and more occupied with my duties. I mentally would not dwell on all of the ramifications of each of these planes containing crew members of real human beings. They were units or packages that were in the wrong place at the wrong time. I would make notations on my charts when a plane went down or pulled away from the formation. I would indicate how many chutes were counted. I tried to ascertain the exact coordinates of where the plane may have crashed and I noted when fighter planes were hit or knocked out of the sky.

My first fears from German fighter planes attacking our formation was on my second mission, which was a particularly long raid to Brux, Czechoslovakia. We were hit by several large groups of fighters midway on our flight to the target and again on our return trip home. At this stage of the aerial war, our fighter planes had a very limited range in which to provide air cover. The German pilots knew this and would hold back until our men were forced to return to England because of their fuel. Then they would usually attack from out of a cloud cover or with the sun at their backs.

The first indication I received through my headset that German fighter planes had been spotted and were attacking immediately brought a knot to my stomach muscles. Even before the planes were within sight, I found myself behind the machine gun on the right side of my small compartment in the B17. I had made up my mind that my left gun was practically useless because of its location, its inability to swing around, and mostly because of the poor visibility from that side. As I stood behind my gun, not knowing what to expect, it became apparent that I had made a huge mistake by firing my gun in their general direction long enough to damage the barrel and jam the gun with an unfired shell. I had forgotten that you were only to fire in 8 second bursts or less, so that the gun would not heat up. Today would be the first and last time I would man these machine guns.

During this long outburst of action, a hot casing was thrown into my left boot and burned my ankle. I saw fighters slashing by my various windows and could do nothing about it. The floor was covered with spent shell casings and I was floundering over these rolling pieces of brass. My throat was so dry that I found it next to impossible to swallow. My head felt like it was in a tight-fitting pail with all of the screaming going on by the various gunners, each reporting a play-by-play account as the Germans made pass after pass. The noise of twelve 50 calibre machine guns being fired simultaneously was added to the sounds generated by the four 1200 hp engines roaring away, making it almost unbearable.

This environment was only part of the total experience. Looking out you could see B-17s fluttering earthward from the group ahead of us. I saw two different German fighters get hit and explode, with pieces of unidentifiable debris flying through the air. Another plane made a lazy arc toward the ground, trailing a beautiful curved column of black smoke. Tracers were skipping and crisscrossing in every direction with little apparent effectiveness. Gunners were screaming into their throat mikes that a plane was coming in at six o'clock low, while another excited voice would announce an attack from ten o'clock high. It was easy to believe that the word calm did not exist.

With a shaky pencil I tried to get as much information down on the margins of the large map spread out on my navigator table. Things were happening so fast and there was so much confusion that it was extremely difficult to spell correctly or to come up with the right words. The brain did not want to function in this living hell. Each of our ten member crew was experiencing combat and this fighter attack for the first time. Fortunately, most of the other planes contained more enlightened crew members that were able to cope with this situation. Each of us in our bomber was trying to deal with an emotion brought on by an experience for which there was no way to prepare.

The unknown is perhaps the worst enemy of the mind. The impact and realization that suddenly you were confronted by someone who was making a maximum effort to kill you, even by putting their own life on the line, has to be a great psychological shock to the system. Each of us had to learn how to live and function with this new experience or we would be reduced to ineffective zombies.

This first air battle took place on the way to our remote target and it ended just as fast as it had begun. The primary difference between how my nerves reacted before and after this first battle was the amount of time it took for my various parts to stop quivering and my chest to resume normal breathing. It took several minutes before I found that I could get my right heel to feel the floor. It felt as though my knee was hinged to move in every direction. Even my pencil took several minutes to calm down so the lead would flow in smooth lines instead of shaky scrawls.

On the return trip from Brux, we were again hit by several dozen fighters. The sound effects were similar and the commotion created was certainly comparable. However, there was a noticeable improvement in the crew in the use of their throat mikes. Screaming had been replaced with excited instructions. The pattern of tracers took on a more effective appearance and I noticed that both of my legs were up to the task of holding me erect. My notes on my chart were more legible, and I welcomed the opportunity to concentrate on my work and to basically ignore the hell going on around me.

The exposure to flak took several additional missions before I was able to keep my emotions under some type of control. This particular tool of war originated at a remote spot nearly five miles below us, and there wasn't a thing that I could do to halt the ensuing explosion of an antiaircraft shell in my midst. I never developed a hatred for the German Luftwaffe pilot, because I respected his courage to attack a formation of bombers, as much as I respected our courage to invade his territory. The flak gunner did not receive this same respect from me because of his remoteness and the fact that his life was not put in equal jeopardy to mine. The anti-aircraft batteries ringed each target and seldom fell victim to our dropped bombs.

These flak gunners knew that each formation of bombers would have a seven or eight minute straight run on the target in order to have the Norden Bomb Sight effective and get the desired bomb pattern. They would shoot up a virtual wall of flak before us and then blanket the entire group on its lengthy trip over the target area. Each shell would explode into thousands of pieces of shrapnel, some the size of half a little finger nail and others the size of your fist. The spinning pieces of raw steel could rip through the thin aluminum skin of the plane and could penetrate anything in its path.

The visual results of these exploding shells were usually huge black puffs of smoke that took on the shape of the letter "Y" tipped on its side or often inverted. The size of these puffs varied, but an average one might be encompassed by a ten foot circle. When these irregular puffs of smoke appeared, the damage had already been done—the shrapnel was on its way in every direction. Most times these shell would be fired at us in clips, with four or five shells leaving the barrel in seconds. From our vantage point, the burst appeared to race toward us. Actually, however, we were flying at them at about 150 miles per hour.

A 128mm flak gun would throw up a shell weighing 87.3 pounds at a velocity of 2,886 feet per second. This gun could fire at the rate of 10 rounds per minute, up to an altitude of over 48,000 feet. A typical important target might be encircled by three or four AA batteries, each of which consisted of six or eight guns. Simple arithmetic would indicate that the Germans were capable of firing in excess of 300 rounds per minute. Any particular Bomber Group could expect to have over two thousand shells explode in its vicinity on a bomb run.

It doesn't take too much imagination to realize the fear that you could muster as you approached this type of danger. Sometimes there were so many puffs of smoke that the area on a bomb run would take on the appearance of a single black cloud. It was dark enough on some occasions that you could actually see the red and yellow colors at the instant of explosion. Sometimes you could look ahead dozens of miles and see the groups ahead being hit. Crew members often joked about the flak being so intense that you could leave the plane and actually walk on it.

You could expect flak at nearly all German targets, but a consistently difficult one that I experienced on several occasions was to Berlin. This city, because of its importance and because of the many prime targets in the immediate area, was especially well protected.

On May l9, 1944, I made my first trip to Berlin. It was only my fourth mission but it was my first real baptism on the effects of flak. There were moments that I found it nearly impossible to breathe; then, there was the fear of having my legs fail me because of extreme trembling. Inside my oxygen mask my lower jaw began to quiver; I felt beads of sweat run into my eyes, even though the temperature in the plane was near 50° below zero. Though you did not want to look, you could not escape the sight of this inferno. I had the feeling that the entire nose of our B-17 was made of clear plexiglass and that I was alone in the center of it. You knew that no other member of the crew could offer help or had the power to change a second of it; it was a complete feeling of helplessness and hopelessness.

During this same bomb run a new experience was also realized. The actual condition of the air became so turbulent from the exploding shells, that each plane bounced and was tossed about. The pilots did their best to maintain the tight formation in order to achieve a better bomb pattern and also to make as small a target as possible. The ride was rough as the B-17 would get pushed upward and just as suddenly drop several feet. An echelon of three planes would be tossed about in an unsynchronized array, sashaying through the sky like three drunken sailors. Fortunately, air sickness was something each of us had mastered long ago.

On this day, I managed to collect four pieces of flak for my growing collection of souvenirs. One piece was retrieved from my right boot when a piece of flak tore through the plywood flooring in my work area, knocking my foot from beneath me. It created a three inch hole in my wool lined leather boot. Another piece of flak ripped through the loose-fitting sleeve of my flight jacket and dropped to the floor—spent. Later, I found a sizable chunk of metal inside my navigator's briefcase where it had damaged several of my navigator books. A fourth piece of flak was headed for my upper torso, but was intercepted by my oxygen line. It made a cut in the tubing and bent away from the wall of the plane, pointing toward me like an arrow. Most of the holes in the nose area were caused by metal fragments that passed right through the plane. After we landed the ground crew quit counting once they got past 150 holes; one was so large that you could drop a basketball through it.

It would be ridiculous to state that a trip such as this, through a hail of flak, would not leave you with frayed nerves and a strong sense of being just plain lucky, once you survived the experience. Little by little though, I did manage to learn to function, keep calm, and perform my duties as a lead navigator. My many responsibilities kept my mind from dwelling on all of the potentials that flak could cause. Instead, I could lose myself in the concentration required in doing my work.

Searching the skies for returning buddies

Ambulances wait for wounded

I soon developed a very strong fatalistic attitude that was perhaps the main reason why I could put the ordeals of a combat mission in a perspective that helped me. I had such strong convictions for my beliefs that I never wore the flak jacket that had been issued. Instead, I gave the co-pilot and the bombardier the two halves of this protective garb. Their desire to protect their "Family Jewels" apparently was as strong as my own beliefs. Also, I never snapped my parachute chest pack to the harness we wore, regardless of the conditions during fighter plane attacks or trips through intense flak. I believed that when my number was intended to be called, it didn't make much difference what I wore or where I was standing.

I will never know the validity of these strong beliefs. I only have the knowledge that I survived a complete tour of duty over the skies of Europe and many more months of flying all over the world while in the Air Transport Command. Most of my friends that were demonstrative about their fears and how they managed to conquer them freely admitted that, as they flew thru hell, they put their complete trust in God, believing that their destiny was in His hands. Others, like myself, were fatalists, with the belief that some law of nature would determine whether we would make it or not, such as "The Law of Probability or the Law of Averages." I knew that my German opponent had the same belief in his God or that he believed as strongly that his cause was just. I firmly believe that there were no staunch atheists flying in any of the 19 different crews with which I flew. At least, I never heard one proclaim this belief. Actually, most men did not talk too much about fear or how they handled it—this really is a very personal thing. To conquer fear required an inner strength that had to be mustered by each individual in his own way.

Two of the original 10 member crew to which I was assigned did not fare as well. Both were officers and after a few missions they were relieved of their duties because of their inability to function properly under combat conditions. I do not know the rate in the Eight Air Force for this type of problem. It is nothing to be ashamed of, since all human beings are different. Each person has their own qualities and capabilities.

Today, millions of people are exposed to man's inhumanity to man. They are compelled to face up to unmentionable fears and horrors beyond description. These are events in which none of us can take pride.

 Nose Art and Nicknames

Nearly all the bombers and fighter planes in the Air Force were given nicknames and most had nose art painted on them by their proud crews. This was a tradition that was started early in the war and rapidly gained momentum as we became more involved. Its beginning was perhaps a modest name or a symbol to indicate fighter kills or missions flown. No one was sure of the attitude that would be taken when it was discovered that government property was decorated against one regulation or another.

Gradually the art work and nicknames progressed into the realm of almost "anything goes." Most of the nose art on B-17s centered around the female form, with little or no clothing, and each was painted in such a way as to exaggerate the curves and delicate lines of these beautiful women. Appropriate names were usually given to these paintings and most were done with a great deal of artistic skill.

I do not know personally of an incident, but I was told that on rare occasions a painting or nickname was censored by the brass because of a lurid pose or because it was too explicit. My own observation indicated that these censors were most lenient. This type of expression by the men who were putting their lives on the line each day was a necessary extension of their feelings. In general, the powers that be knew this.

This harmless expression, regardless of the message conveyed, seemed to be necessary to the individuals involved. Obviously, a bold or suggestive nickname or an exotic nude woman painted on the nose of a plane could do nothing to ward off a German fighter plane or the devastating flak barrages that each plane experienced. The importance to the flight crews and their ground personnel was that they were drawn closer together by the pride that they took in their plane. Giving their machine for war a name and a "trademark" made it more personal and seemed to give their "baby" its own personality.

The original B-17 crew to which I was assigned was very typical, and the name and nose art we developed is indicative of how this tradition became famous in the Eighth Air Force. Shortly after we (ten individuals, from eight different states and all walks of life) were assigned to a crew, we were issued a new shiny silver Flying Fortress. We all agreed that our plane should have a name and be decorated with nose art.

My best friend and our co-pilot, Dan Waddell, had just gotten married. He and his wife, Claire, took a two-day honeymoon to Omaha, Nebraska, not far from Grand Island, the base to which we were assigned. Dan brought back an interesting napkin from the White Horse Bar in Omaha. It was a napkin with a picture of a cute little gal that seemed to appeal to all crew members. It was mutually agreed that this was the figure that we wanted to be painted on our A-2 leather jackets and on the nose of our new B-17G, which was the latest bomber complete with chin turret and other new innovations.

We all felt that the name on the napkin "LADY LUCK" was too common and would be used by other crews. We wanted something really different. At this time on this and other bases, the phrase "hard luck" was often heard whenever anyone made a statement seeking a small degree of sympathy. We decided that the word *hard* would be drawn out with a very broad "A" sound. It does not make much sense today as I write this, but at the moment it seemed to express our feelings and attitudes. For some ridiculous reason we all decided to defy the implications that "HAARD LUCK" conjured up and would use this as our nickname. With some difficulty, I managed to track down some oil paints and a few art brushes. With a sketch pad, I drew our newfound young lady to a scale that was suitable for my A-2 leather jacket and proceeded to transfer this work of art, along with the name "HAARD LUCK" and the 95th Bomb Group Logo onto my jacket. I had a fair degree of artistic talent so the results turned out well. One by one the other crew members prevailed upon me to paint their jackets. Repeating this assignment ten times was no small task, took many weeks of work, and used up most of my spare moments. I enjoyed the challenge and the knowledge of what this meant to my fellow crew members.

It was more difficult to find the time to actually work on the nose of old number 297334 at the "hardstand." It required working on a ladder and most days the weather did not cooperate. For a variety of reasons, I never finished the work, even on one side. On several missions, the picture received flak damage and had to have aluminum patches riveted to the skin. Moreover, several different crews were flying 297334 and they were not thrilled with the name that we had chosen. On May 24th, as our plane was returning to our base at Horham, England, from an aborted mission, Lt. Cobb came in hot, braked too hard, blew a right tire, ground looped, collapsed the right landing gear, and tore up the right wing. Our plane was in repairs for nearly two months, during which time all signs of my art work had been removed. Lt. Cobb was demoted and I moved on to be a lead navigator with many different crews.

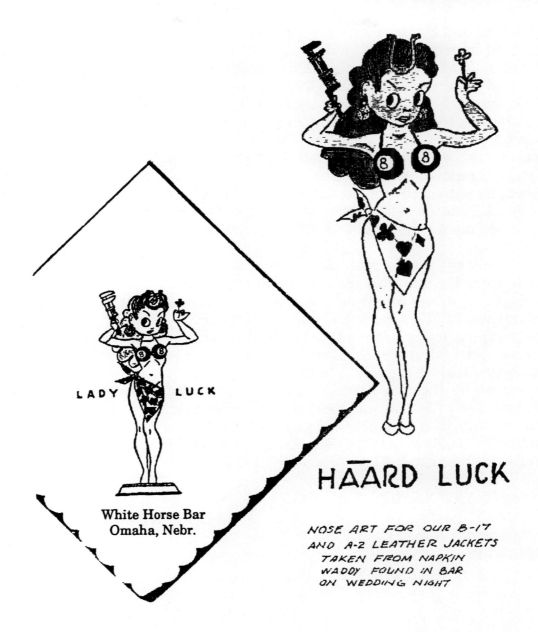

HAARD LUCK

NOSE ART FOR OUR B-17
AND A-2 LEATHER JACKETS
TAKEN FROM NAPKIN
WADDY FOUND IN BAR
ON WEDDING NIGHT

White Horse Bar
Omaha, Nebr.

Many felt that because of the name "HAARD LUCK," our plane and crew had been hexed. I guess there is no way of really knowing if old No. 297334 sustained worse treatment because of its name. This B-17 went on to complete 41 combat missions, was flown by 20 different pilots, and was finally shot down on September 11, 1944. The average life of a B-17 in the 95th bomber group was 33.2 combat missions.

I wore my A-2 jacket through the entire war and completed my 35 combat missions. The rest of my original crew did not fare as well. The first pilot and bombardier were not able to withstand combat and were relieved from duty. My best friend, Waddell, the co-pilot, was wounded October 17th on his 31st mission and was shipped home. Several of the enlisted men received wounds but I'm not sure if any actually finished their tour of duty. Luck, like beauty, is in the eye of the beholder. During the war I was a staunch fatalist, believing that when one's number was up, regardless of nose art, nicknames, or thousands of other idiosyncrasies, one would meet his destiny whatever it might be. My new A-2 Jacket is painted with the name "HAARD LUCK," along with 35 small bombs indicating the missions that I have completed. The original jacket suffered from the salt spray of the Atlantic Ocean, which resulted from my standing on the bridge of the Queen Mary on my way back to the U.S.A.

The following table contains the nose art names of the planes of the 95th Bomb Group. This most impressive list contains the Squadron of each plane, its serial number, and the actual nose art names in alphabetical order. There were many duplications of certain names because of their popularity or perhaps for some sentimental reason. Also, a few planes had several names given throughout their service because different crews took them over. Because most of these planes were either destroyed by German fighter planes or flak or were destroyed by our government after the war, less than a dozen examples remain today. Fortunately, many pictures were taken of the famous art work displayed on the thousands of B-17s, B-24s, attack bombers, and many of the fighter planes such as the P-47, P-38, and the P-51.

NOSE ART NAMES, 95th B.G.

Sqadron Number	Air Craft Number	Name on Plane
334	42-31920	Able Mable
412	42-37882	A Good Bet
		Angle Of Destruction
336	42-30167	Angel's Pumpkin
336	42-30176	Assassin
412	42-97376	Aunt Callie's Baby
412	42-37876	Batcha's Patches
412	43-37898	Belle In The Keyhole
335	43-38942	Belligerent Beauty
336	42-31410	Berlin Bessie
412	42-31675	Berlin Bessie
335	42-32002	Berlin First

Sqadron Number	Air Craft Number	Name on Plane
334	43-38229	Better Duck
335	42-31887	Big Casino
412	43-38067	Big Chief Illiniwok
334	42-31989	Black Magic
334	41-23202	Blondie
334	42-30182	Blondie II
412	44-6946	Blood & Guts
412	42-37882	Blues In The Reich
335	42-30271	BomBoggie
		Bouncing Bitch
334	41-25986	Brown's Mule
		Cadet Nurse
335	43-38814	Cadet Nurse the 2nd
335	44-6838	Cal's Rascals
335	41-23089	Captain Eddie
412	42-29919	Carondale Special
412	42-97858	Carmen's Folly
336	42-29811	Chattanooga Choo Choo
		Cheri
412	42-31999	Chicken Ship
336	42-30674	Cincinnati Queen
412	42-30173	Circe
335	42-30161	Cuddle Cat
336	42-37734	Cuddle Cat
335	42-30178	Darlin' Dolly
		Dawnbuster
334	42-107050	Deltress
412	43-38744	Der Fuehrer's Nightmare
336	42-30167	Destony's Tot
336	42-30674	Destiny's Tot
334	42-31057	Devil's Daughter the 2nd
335	42-37929	Dianna
412	44-46522	Dirty Duchess
335	42-38140	Dolly's Daughter
		Dream Baby
		Easy Aces
334	42-102447	El's Belles
336	42-38140	E.T.O. Happy
412	43-38657	Evasive Action
335	43-38346	Excellsior

Sqadron Number	Air Craft Number	Name on Plane
412	42-30150	Exterminator
334	42-3004 5	Fight' n-n-Bitin'
412	42-31876	Fire Ball
412	42-31876	Fire Ball Red
336	42-37988	Flagship
		Flak Happy
		Floozie Flossie
335	42-30272	Fritz Blitz
335	42-31514	Full House
412	42-97797	Full House
		Furlong
412	42-97232	G. I. Issue
334	42-31993	Genril Oop
336	42-107204	Going My Way
412	43-38288	Going My Way
412	42-97232	Government Property
336	42-97334	**HAARD LUCK**
334	42-38054	Hamawa
	41-9021	Hangar Queen
412	42-97992	Hap Hazard
412	42-37882	Hard Time
		Harley Charley
412	42-39869	Heaven Can Wait
336	41-25918	Heavenly Daze
		Heavy Date
334	42-30300	Hell-n-Back
335	44-8144	Hell's Belle
		Herky Jerky
335	42-30181	Herky Jerky II
		Hi Voltage
412	42-38054	Holy Matrimony
336	42-30244	Holy Terror
334	42-31760	Ikky Poo
336	42-31410	I Dood It
412	42-31320	I '11 Be Around
412	41-23273	Impatient Virgin
412	42-31054	Irish Luck
412	44-6522	It Flies
		Jeanie
412	43-38067	Joyride

Sqadron Number	Air Craft Number	Name on Plane
334	42-31299	Junior
		Just Elmer's Tune
336	42-29703	Kathy Jane
336	41-23321	Kathy Jane II
336	42-30674	Kathy Jane III
412	43-38281	Kimmie Kar
412	42-97257	Knock-Out-Baby
334	43-38346	Kurchow
		Lackanookie
412	42-97858	Lady Fortune
412	42-30322	Liberty Belle
412	42-30634	Liberty Belle
336	42-38127	Liberty Ship
334	41-23194	Little Hell
334	42-29791	Little Jimmie
		Little Jo
		Little Lady
		Little Nell
		Lonesome Polecat
412	42-30255	Lonesome Polecat II
412	42-29737	Louise
412	42-30288	Louise II
335	42-30181	Lover Boy
412	43-37783	Lueky Sherry
334	42-31258	Lueky Strike
		Lu Lu
335	43-38760	Lucky Lady
335	42-102455	Lucky Lady II
335	42-97376	Lucky Lady III
		Magnificent Obsession
335	42-6080	Mary Ruth the "WeWa" Special
336	42-29754	Mason's Morons
336	42-30283	Mason's Morons
334	42-31992	Mirrandy
		Miss Flower
		Miss Flower II
334	42-30817	Miss Flower III
412	42-37976	Miss Raps-O-Dee
		Mr. Fly By Fly
		Natsha

Sqadron Number	Air Craft Number	Name on Plane
412	42-37976	New York Express
		No Excuse
334	42-31924	Ol' Dog
		Ol' Dog II
335	41-23046	Ol' Jackson-That Frisco Kid
334	42-102678	Ole Worrybird
335	42-30274	Our Bay-Bee
336	42-102450	Paisano
412	42-29706	Passion Flower
334	42-30120	Patches
412	42-30322	Patches
334	42-29807	Patsy Ann
		Patsy Ann II
334	42-30273	Patsy Ann III
		Pegasus
		Pegasus II
		Pegasus III
334	42-37894	Pegasus IV
412	41-23095	Peggy Ann
334	42-30418	Picadilly Commando
412	42-31999	Pickwickian
335	42-30609	Pistol Packing Mama
334	42-31600	Pride of New Mexico
335	42-37889	Pride of Vhelhalis
334	42-107154	Puddles
		Pug
		Queen Mary
336	42-29702	Rat Killer
412	42-102937	Ready Freddie
412	42-30233	Rapsody On Flak
335	42-31462	Roarin' Bill
335	42-37756	Roarin' Bill
		Roger The Dodger
		Roger The Lodger
412	42-30377	Roger The Lodger II
334	42-25791	Ruthless
		Ryan's Boys
		Sack Robber
		Sad Sack
336	41-23462	San Antonio Rose

Sqadron Number	Air Craft Number	Name on Plane
335	42-102455	Screeming Eagle
		Sentimental Value
334	42-30045	She's My Gal
334	42-31299	She's My Gal II
335	42-97264	Shoo Shoo Baby
		Silver Dollar
334	42-29780	Silver Queen
412	42-32066	Silver Slipper
334	42-29943	Situation Normal
335	41-23266	Sitting Bull
		Sleepy Time Gal
335	41-23263	Slightly Dangerous
412	42-30105	Slightly Dangerous
335	42-31785	Slightly Dangerous II
334	42-97290	Smiling Sandy Sanchez
412	44-6522	SNAFU
412	42-29694	Southern Belle
		Spare Parts
		Spirit Of Martinez
334	42-316001	Spirit Of New Mexico
336	42-29704	Spook
336	41-23176	Spook II
336	42-5882	Spook III
336	42-30286	Spook IV
336	42-30266	Spook #5
335	42-31063	Spook Six
		Stacie's Special
412	42-107204	Stand By
		Starduster
		Stinky
		Strickly Zoot
412	42-37876	Struggle Buggy
335	42-6098	Superstitious Aloysius
412	44-6522	Sweet Jo
336	42-29705	Sweet 17
335	44-8210	Sweetheart Of Seattle
		Tailbait
412	42-30342	Taint A Bird
		Taint A Bird II
335	43-37783	Temptation

Sqadron Number	Air Craft Number	Name on Plane
335	43-37783	Ten Aces
335	42-30353	Ten Knights In The Bar Room
336	42-30276	Terry And The Pirates
334	42-102560	The Thomper
412	44-8040	13th Jinx
334	42-38123	To Hell Or Glory
412	42-29740	Tondelayo
334	42-39924	Toranado
334	42-107050	Toranado Jr.
335	42-97992	Trouble Buggy
334	42-30135	Trouble Shooter
412	44-6801	Umbriago
412	43-38288	V For Victory
		Victory Devils
		Virgin On The Verg
335	42-30194	Wee Ain't Scared
412	42-30185	Wee Bonnie
		Wee Miss America
		Wha-Whoo
		What's Cooking
334	42-29787	Wilder Nell
412	44-8741	Winged Warriors
334	42-29768	Winsome Winn
334	42-107201	Worry Bird
335	42-37879	Wrinkled Belly Baby
336	41-23283	Yankee Queen
335	42-29709	Yo' Brother

(The following are not in order)

412	42-39177	(the) Blessed Event
		(the) Blivit
335	41-23111	(the) Brass Rail
336	41-23153	(the) Devil's Daughter
334	42-107047	(the) Doodle Bug
334	41-23400	(the) Gremlin's Sweetheart
		(the) Holy Terrors
		(the) Mad Medic
336	42-38140	(the) Pregnant Goose
		(the) Snake Charmer
412	41-23317	(the) Spirit Of 76
412	42-30235	(the) Zoot Suiters

It is obvious that the names on the noses of the B-17s in the 95th B.G. fell into several categories. The following are examples:
1. Those who honored a loved one: Darlin Dollie; Cheri; Dianna; Kathy Jane; Patsy Ann or Louise.
2. Those who tried to be clever or cute: Batch's Patches Dawn Busters; Roger the Dodger; Sack Robber; or Situation Normal.
3. Those who defied fate or the Germans: HAARD LUCK; Flak Happy; SNAFU; 13th Jinx, or Assassin
4. Those who tried to be promiscuous: Virgin on the Verg; Lackanookie; Tailbait; Impatient Virgin, etc.

The Curtain Drops

Finally, September 5, 1944, and the day of my 35th mission. This is the mission each airman of a bomber crew looks forward to and also the one he fears the most. No one wants to go down during any raid, but particularly his very last one. I knew the night before that I was scheduled to fly as lead navigator for this particular mission, but I would have to wait to find out where the target would be.

A very restless night was spent, thinking about going home soon, hoping this last trip to Germany would turn out successful, and finally bringing to an end a most exciting chapter in my young life. I knew that the time that I had spent in combat would be like no other experience. Now that I could see the end to my tour, I believed that it was possible for me to close this period and return home with both a sound and whole body and mind.

On the morning of the 5th, I discovered at briefing that my last mission was scheduled against a target at Stuttgart, Germany, a factory complex. I had flown my 23rd mission to this same city on July 16th, less than two months ago, so I had some idea of what to expect. We all knew that the flak would be intense, to put it mildly. Stuttgart is located some what in a valley, has a population of nearly 700,000 people, and had many industrial plants. Because of its importance to the German war effort, the city was ringed with flak batteries. Each of these flak batteries had eight 88mm or 105mm guns. The railroad batteries each had four 105mm guns.

I had flown as a lead navigator with 19 different crews on 20 some of my 35 missions, so today's endeavor would be fairly routine, especially in the knowledge of what we could expect along the route going to and returning from our target. I guess the only unusual feeling I had this particular day was that this, one way or another, would be my last trip against an enemy for whom I felt no real hatred. I later learned that my German opponent in these skies over Europe felt very similar. We both did what we had been trained to do with no real animosity.

All 38 B-17s took off in 30 second intervals on this cool, crisp, and clear morning. In short order we headed for Buncher 7 and proceeded to get into formation. About this time, Lt. P. A. Kross pulled away from the Group stating that his fuel gauge instruments had failed and that he was returning to our Base at Horham. Before we started crossing the Channel, we had joined the 100th Bomb Group and the 390th Bomb Group, which made up the 13th Bomber Wing. Just about this time, Lt. W.G. Helm and his crew reported that their propeller governor oil line had broken and that they also would be returning to base. Thirty six Bombers would make up the 95th today for our trip to the middle of Germany.

Our landfall on the Continent was just south of Antwerp, Netherlands; and our course was intentionally chosen to look like we were going to bomb Frankfurt, Germany. As we passed a few miles south of Koblenz, we altered course and headed toward Stuttgart. Passing south of Frankfurt, we could see the flak they had thrown up in anticipation of a raid. This was our greeting if we wanted to go to their city. Their turn would come another day.

We could see hundreds of our "Little Friends" on each side of our formation and the Groups ahead and behind us. These P-51s, 47s, and P-38s were always welcomed, and we felt secure today that no German fighter plane would try to challenge us. At this point in the war, our fighters had gained over a 10 to 1 kill ratio—odds that were most impressive.

As we approached our I. P. Point near Pforzheim our run into the target, all of our fighters pulled back to avoid the expected flak. They knew that the Germans would not send their fighters into this hazard and they knew that their presence would not help our cause. The Germans did not disappoint us. Eight minutes out from "Bombs Away," we turned on a heading of 110°. The wall of flak was awaiting us and we were soon boxed in with flak on each side and in front of us along our predetermined course. It was awesome. You almost had the feeling that you were passing through a black turbulent cloud.

By now we had gained considerable advantage over the Germans with our fighter coverage and with the number of heavy bombers that we could put up. At the same time, German anti-aircraft gunners had improved with better radar equipment and now most of the 88mm gun had been replaced with 105mm improved weapons. These gunners had a wealth of experience and could accurately find the right altitude for their shells to explode. Our only choice was to weather their efforts and place our bombs on the targets picked out by our commanders.

Once the 95th dropped their load of 144,000 pounds of bombs, we turned tail on a heading of 290° to get the hell away from the flak. Nearly all of our planes had been hit by pieces of these flak shells in varying degrees. However, Lt. J. L. Walker reported in to our plane that he had two engines out and could not hold altitude or his position in the formation. Fortunately, our fighter escort picked up the same message as they were waiting for our emergence from the target area. Several P-51s circled the B-17 No. 338106 and escorted it to a safe landing behind our lines in France. He and his crew made it back to our base and were able to return to combat on September 9th, just four days later.

As we approached the English Channel, I noticed that the course we were on was going to take us over the Belgium city of Oostende on the coast. I remembered reading in the Stars and Stripes that many of these coastal cities were by-passed by the Allied Forces and were to be mopped-up later. They had German troops with their weapons. I informed my pilot, Lt. Griffin about my concern and that he should direct the entire formation to alter course to avoid this city. Since we were a lead ship, we had a Colonel flying as co-pilot. He immediately broke in to our conversation and stated that our present course would take us to our Base at Horham and that we would not delay our arrival by altering course. His wish was my command.

We flew over this little Belgium town, received some flak, and picked up some additional battle damage. This entire incident is only mentioned because later that day I would be "called on the carpet" over this matter. No one was seriously hurt, and I never thought much about this stupid decision. I will elaborate on the outcome of this incident later.

We arrived back at Horham with 13 planes badly hit; many had several wounded personnel aboard. Our Group was one of the luckier ones. Many of our friends from other Groups went down with their planes. Once our wheels touched down, I knew that I was finished with my 35th and last mission. Thirty-five does not seem like a huge number; but as you fly these missions one at a time, many like today's effort, you begin to see just how relative everything is. I truly was grateful to have survived these trips into Germany, the Netherlands, Belgium, Denmark, France, and even Czechoslovakia. I had a cigar box filled with pieces of flak that I had collected from my clothing, my boots, my navigational equipment, and from the immediate area around me. I knew that any one of these pieces of steel could have had my name on it. The only injury I had received during my entire tour was a simple face wound from flying Plexiglass when my astro-dome was shattered. I knew just how fortunate I was to have survived a complete tour of combat.

My plans for the time immediately after I flew my last mission was to tap a fifth of brandy that I had been saving just for this most auspicious occasion and get plowed. However, this was not the feeling that I was experiencing at this moment. Inside, I knew that I had made it despite tremendous odds and that the word grateful was not enough. My friends were all happy; but most importantly, they informed me that I was scheduled to be shipped home the day after tomorrow. For some reason, I found myself walking over to the N.C.O. Club, a place I had never been in before this evening, to visit some of the many enlisted men I had flown with on these 19 different crews. I had a few beers with them when I received notice that I was wanted on the double at headquarters. They had been looking for me for over an hour. I ran to headquarters and found Col. Truesdell and three other officers impatiently awaiting my arrival. Colonel Truesdell asked me why in hell I had taken the 95th over Oostende. With a sinking feeling, I informed him and the others that I had told Lt. Griffin about the potential flak and was overruled by Col. "So and So," and he ordered me to stay on the existing course. Much to my amazement, Col. Truesdell simply said, "that's all I need to know, congratulations on completing your missions Krueger, and good luck in the future." I left feeling someone was going to get their tail chewed out.

Years later, back in December 26, 1951, I had the great fortune to meet a former German fighter pilot who just happened to be from Stuttgart, Germany. He had been in the war since 1939 and fought in the Battle of Britain, was shot down twice over German soil so he could return to action, and was finally put out of the war by one of our P-51s in 1944 and taken prisoner. The reason I relate this friendship is that on the day of my last mission to Stuttgart, his home near the target area was damaged and caught fire. We both thought that this was quite a coincidence that we, who were forced to fight one another, should by chance get to meet and become friends. These past 39 years he has visited our home twice and we have been to Germany and his home twice. We exchange letters on a monthly basis.

When we visited Stuttgart in 1989, we saw signs of the damage that the Allied bombing had inflicted on this large city. The place had sustained 52 bombing raids by the 8th Air Force and was 45 percent destroyed. Two of my 35 missions were targets in Stuttgart. After the war, the German people began cleaning up the rubble and reconstructing their buildings. All or most of this mess was trucked to a distant site on the edge of the city and was eventually made into a park and memorial. Millions of loads of broken bricks, plaster, stone, and other material were delivered to this site and methodically unloaded in a conical shaped mountain. After the city had been cleaned up, they trucked black dirt to this huge hill and covered the slopes, planted thousand of trees, and carved a winding, spiral path to the summit. On the plateau on the top, identifiable rubble was left exposed, such as column caps, arches, stone carvings, and so forth. A huge wooden cross was erected and several benches

Stuttgart, Germany - 1989
45 years after last mission

were placed so that you could look down on Stuttgart from the top of this small mountain.

As I sat and meditated, it was not difficult to realize that man never profits from past experiences. Less than 25 years earlier, another war swept this land, leaving death and destruction in its wake. It is all so senseless.

Returning Home

It is September 5, 1944, and my 35th combat mission is now behind me. The last mission to Stuttgart had been rough. My day began at 4:30 A.M., and my body was buzzing with unfamiliar anxieties. When I finally went to bed on this auspicious night, I had mixed emotions. As I stared off into the darkness, I had feelings of gratitude for surviving my tour of duty here in England. These thoughts were intermingled with memories of my many friends that either had cashed in their chips or who had many missions to fly. I was about to go home and leave these buddies behind.

My relationship with Lt. Dan Waddell was more than two guys being thrown together by fate, one from North Carolina and one from Wisconsin, one from the South and one from the North. Our friendship was instant, genuine, and came at a most important time in both of our lives. All of our interests were similar and it was seldom that we were apart during our free moments. We started out on the same bomber crew but got split up by outside forces. Our bunks were together, so we were in constant communication with one another. Tonight it hit me for the first time that our friendship would be split up by my leaving and that it would be a long time before we ever got a chance to see one another again. I also knew that "Waddy" had only reached his 24th mission and that he still had 11 big ones to go. Thoughts and fears entered my head, greater worries than I had for any of my pending trips to Germany.

Note: "Waddy was later wounded on his 31st. mission on October 17, 1944, and would not be compelled to finish the required 35." Our paths never crossed again while we were in the service. After the war we exchanged notes on Christmas cards and occasional letters. In 1959, Norma and I took a trip to Hendersonville, N.C., to visit Dan and Claire Waddell. Since then we have gotten together on several occasions.

My thoughts on this memorable night raced home and the realization that Norma and I were going to be married. I suddenly became aware of the fact that all of our courtship had been via the mails. Just before I left for combat, we had become engaged, but all of our thoughts, promises, and dreams for the future were communicated through letters. Even my proposal for marriage had to be done on cheap paper with some censor receiving the news before Norma. Serious thoughts crept into these moments that made me realize that the touching, the hugs and kisses, the expressions, the deep inner thoughts and all of the other things that go into normal relationships had been missing. There never was any doubt that I had located the person who I wanted to spend and share my life with. Only, this night I wanted to know more about her dreams and wishes and whether I was the right person for her. I knew that if the next eight months were to be as interesting and exciting as the past eight months, then we would have it made.

Another interesting picture kept popping into my mind. I knew my days in the Air Corps were not over. The war continued and my services were still required. Where would I be stationed and what would my duties be? I had been told of several options that might be available but each depended on openings and being in the right place at the right time. I shall always remember this lengthy night when a myriad of thoughts raced through my mind.

On Wednesday morning, September 6th, I had to hand in all of my navigational equipment and sign a lot of official papers and forms for my discharge from combat duty and my return to the States. I was asked to address a group of new navigators to let them know what to expect on actual combat missions, how to be effective, and to answer any questions they might have. As I spoke and looked into their anxious faces, I could hardly believe that just eight months ago I too wondered what combat would be like and had the unreal hope that the war would not be over before I could get into it. This hope will immediately vanish for them after the first trip across the English Channel.

Today is Thursday and I get some good news and some bad. I was informed that I would leave the 95th Bomb Group Base here at Horham, England, tomorrow morning and be shipped to Glasgow, Scotland, to board the Queen Mary for my trip home. The negative news had to do with a good friend of mine, Captain Lyle Dallman, our Group Navigator from Antigo, Wisconsin. He had volunteered to go on a shuttle mission that would take our Group from England to Russia; Russia to Italy; and Italy back to England. Enroute, three deep air strikes would be dealt to the Germans, an interesting concept. Lyle had left over a week ago. Before he had left he had given me several items to take home to his wife in Antigo, Wisconsin, such as his war medals, and other mementoes. Just a few moments after I got the news about the Queen Mary, I was told that the lead plane had been shot down over Hungary while enroute to Italy. Our Base only knew at that time that the plane was missing.

Early Friday morning I joined Lt. Richard Harvey and the entire crew for our return to the States. I knew all ten of the members of this crew and was happy to be traveling with familiar faces. The eleven of us were trucked to the railroad station at Diss, a small English town northwest of Horham. In less than a half hour we boarded a train to Glasgow, Scotland. For the first time, all of us became very talkative and were just beginning to believe this was all true. We arrived late at night and were quartered in a hotel that the U.S. Government had taken over. We did a fair share of celebrating before the day was brought to an end.

Saturday morning we were told that we would not board the ship until 8 P.M. that evening. In the meantime, I placed a call to the 95th Base to check if any further information was received concerning the plane that was shot down. Several crews that had made it to Italy reported that Capt. Dallman and the other members of the lead B-17 were seen parachuting from the burning plane before it exploded. Their target had been a railroad shop in Szolnok, Hungary. Now, at least, I could inform Dorothy Dallman that her husband was alive and that he was a P.O.W. instead of "Missing in Action" with no other information forthcoming for many months.

The 9th of September was an especially long day, even for a Saturday. We walked the streets, we drank, we walked some more, we drank. We did this until it got almost dark. About 6 P.M. we all piled into two taxicabs and headed for the dock at Gourock. Hundreds of Americans were already lined up, waiting to board the biggest ship these eyes have ever seen. The harbor was at the mouth of the Clyde River in Scotland and it emptied into the Firth of Clyde where the Mighty Queen was anchored. Dozens of ambulances could be seen, and we were told that they had been loading wounded soldiers from the war since before noon. Excitement permeated the air. Just before our group was to board the ship, a G.I., who was starting to go up the gang plank, offered me a whole, large, cooked red lobster. Being from Wisconsin, I didn't know what this ghastly looking creature would taste like. Much to his amazement I turned down his generous offer. Before he got out of arms reach, he tore off one huge claw and told me to try it. I looked at it long and hard and was not quite sure about how to attack it. I finally and cautiously tasted this strange edible monster. It was succulent. Once I got on board, I raced around the upper deck trying without success to find this generous G.I.

I had been assigned, along with seven other officers, to a 1st Class stateroom on the veranda deck. It was a huge room with 12 single beds in it. Only the eight of us shared this ample space for the next six days.

166 • Returning Home

The three greatest liners ever built are docked together for the only time, in 1940. Sharing the Cunard Pier with the twin-stacked Queen Elizabeth is the triple-stacked Queen Mary. Beyond her lies the elegant Normandie, pride of the French line.

Queen Mary

Later, I was told that this stateroom would cost a family $2,000 for a single crossing.

The Queen Mary is one hell of a ship. In normal times 1,904 passengers would sail with a crew of 1,285. Now this ship was serving its country in the time of war. All of the luxury trappings had been removed. Six miles of carpeting, 220 cases of china, crystal, and silver were in storage in a warehouse. As a troop carrier, she normally would carry between 14,000 and 16,000 troops. This return trip to the United States would have fewer than 3,000 passengers, made up of mostly wounded, several hundred Air Corp Personnel, several hundred ground troops returning home on leave, and an unusual contingent of pregnant WACS, WAVES, and Nurses.

The Queen Mary was launched in 1934 and was one of the prime ships in the world. Her sister ship, the Queen Elizabeth, was under construction at the beginning of the war and would be 12 feet longer and slightly heavier than the 81,237 gross tons the Queen Mary weighed. Four sets of single-reduction- geared turbines ran the ship. Each developed 160,000 shaft horsepower that drove the four 18 foot propellers. Normal speed was about 27 knots per hour, which meant that the ship would consume over 1,000 tons of fuel every 24 hours. Instead of the normal crew of 1,285, she now was run by only 200. The ship was 1,019 feet long, approximately one-fifth of a mile in length or the equivalent of 3.5 football fields.

The Queen Mary went into service for the war effort on April 17, 1940. She had been refitted to bring American and Canadian troops to England as rapidly as possible. In all , she made a total of 89 crossings. One of the wars most memorable brief log entries went as follows:

"New York to Gourock (Clyde), 16,683 souls aboard. New York 25 July, 1943, Gourock 30 July, 1943, 3,353 miles, 4 days, 20 hours, 42 minutes, 28.173 knots. The greatest number of human beings ever embarked on one vessel." That says it all.

To carry these huge numbers of troops, standee bunks were developed. It was a tree of metal tubes supporting six canvas stretchers to accommodate six sleeping soldiers. On the Observation Lounge it was converted into a maze of five-tiered bunks. Each normal cabin, instead of a single couple, was fitted with 18 triple-tiered units for 54 men. When 16,000 men were transported, 3 G.I.s rotated shifts in each bunk over a 24-hour period. Meals were served 2,000 at a time, starting at 6:30 A.M.. 30,000 eggs were boiled every morning, just to give some idea of the magnitude of the food problem. The Queen was fitted with some armament for these crossings. A total of 40 guns made up of 12 rocket launchers and some anti-aircraft cannons. These were never used.

168 • Returning Home

The Seafarers. The Great Liners by Melvin Maddocks and Time-Life Books.

This is a picture of the Queen Mary loaded with over 16,000 troops on their way to England. This famous ship made 89 crossings for her contribution for the war effort. There were approximately 3,000 passengers when I returned in September, 1944.

My first impression of this majestic ship was that she was a floating city with restaurants, banks, hospitals, theaters, and all of the other pertinences. Since we had only about one-fifth of the number of passengers on this return trip, my impressions are bound to be somewhat different from those G.I.s that left New York for their war. In all of my excitement, I walked the decks continuously for six or seven hours, trying to see and learn as much as possible about this beautiful "Lady." I got lost several dozen times, sometimes many decks below.

We slowly left the dock about 11 P.M. and did not reach the open sea, north of Ireland, till early the next morning. I spent so much time near the bow of the ship watching the water or just soaking in the feeling and spirit of the trip that ever so slowly my leather A-2 flight jacket absorbed the moist salt spray. Later, when I tried to get this mottled white salt out of my treasured jacket, I found that it had been ruined. The leather just disintegrated.

As a navigator, I soon discovered by watching the stars at night, that the Queen Mary was constantly altering course in a very erratic way. This, I was told, was done so that no German U-Boat could intercept us. The Queen was faster than any submarine, but it would have been suicide to head in a straight line for New York because it could have been intercepted. It had been learned that Hitler had offered $250,000 and an Iron Cross to any U-Boat captain who sank one of the two Queens.

On Monday night, September 11th, I went up to the bridge and asked if I could peek into the ship's navigator's area. To my amazement, I was invited in and had the opportunity to work with the ship's navigator for several hours. I took star shots and helped plot the resulting fixes. In an airplane, when practicing celestial navigation, we had to shoot three stars about 120° apart in a period of ten minutes. We then moved the first star shot up 5 minutes in time and the last star shot back 5 minutes. On board ship we could take a half hour to shoot these three stars on a very calm deck and we did not have to alter any of the data. The reason for this is that a ship moves thru the water at about one-tenth the speed of our B-17.

As an officer, I was assigned to Officer Of The Day duties, which meant that I spent several hours below deck in the hospital sick bay areas where the seriously wounded were kept. I saw things that I hardly was prepared for. Men without arms and legs, faces partially blown away, various degrees of bandaging and traction devices filled beds in many different bays. Despite this horrible and sad picture, most of the men were in very high spirits. We talked and swapped war stories. Many told me that there was no way you could get one of them into an airplane, let alone face German fighter planes or enemy flak. I told them that there was no way you could get me into a tank, or a submarine, or even a trench. I guess it took all types of Americans to win this terrible war. Once again, I realized just how fortunate I was to come home in one piece.

Three days out from England, several of my friends and I got the D.T.'s. (dementia tremors). We had heard that there would be severe disciplinary action taken if anyone was caught bringing alcohol on board the Queen Mary. The net result was that we drank our intended supply before we boarded. They did a good job of checking. Now it was the 12th and we were hard put for just one good drink. We had found out that Bing Crosby and Fred Astaire were on this trip, going home from a recent U.S.O. show they had put on for the troops in France and England. They had put on a show aboard ship for the wounded but refused to do the same for the able bodied passengers. The plan was to contact either one of these Hollywood celebrities and ask if we could buy a bottle of any kind of booze. After arguing for several minutes, we decided all three of us would knock on Crosby's stateroom door and present the question. Much to Lt. Lyons, Lt. Evans, and Lt. Kruegers' amazement, we were invited in. We were ushered over to a well-stocked bar and were told to mix our own "poison." We sat around and talked for some time, had several drinks, and were asked if we knew how to play poker. The only three things that each of us had done in the past eight months was fly, drink, and play poker for money. Say no more.

The stakes in this poker game were modest—a dollar to call a card, for example, instead of the British Pound with which we were accustomed to playing. (Note: a British Pound was worth $4.035 back in 1944). The most memorable thing about this special evening was not the card game, nor the fact that our systems were getting the alcohol that they craved, nor the fact that I even made a few bucks from the game, nor was it the fact that we were in the presence of two of our countries most notable entertainers. No, it was that these two famous people came across as two simple, ordinary guys. They made us feel at ease and comfortable. We immediately called them Fred and Bing, not out of disrespect, but rather because we sensed that this is what they preferred. They directed all of the conversation in the direction of what each of us did in our respective crews and what some of our experiences were in combat. We were made to feel welcome and the three of us did our best to express our appreciation for this most memorable evening. I learned this night that Fred Astaire wore a wig that was left on his dresser. They both made me feel very young. We left their smoke-filled state room with an experience each of us will cherish and long remember. I have to believe that we left these two Hollywood Joes with a similar feeling.

Now that I had my motor purring along in good fashion, I could now get back to enjoying the trip. Each day the weather was perfect (not the usual condition in the Atlantic), and we could see stars almost every night. Early on the morning of September 15th, a Friday, we entered the harbor in New York, passed through the narrows between Staten Island and Long Island and entered Upper Bay. Many small boats darted around us. There were several fire boats spraying water into lazy arcs while several small tugs were maneuvering next to the hull of this huge ship. Each minute brought troops up from the lower decks to find room along the rails. By mid-morning we could see Ellis Island and the Statue of Liberty. Tears filled most of our eyes as the reality of reaching home began to sink in. We slowly moved up the Hudson River with Manhattan to our starboard. Excitement was not the word for it. This fellow from a little town in Wisconsin was standing on the deck of one of the world's greatest ships and moving gracefully in the harbor of the world's greatest city. As we inched our way into Cunards Pier No. 89, we were greeted by a large band and thousands of waving people. I felt a special pride in being an American, and I knew what I had risked my neck in combat for. The memory of this entire scene is what my country is all about.

It took hours before I could leave the ship, but this didn't seem to matter today. I soaked in all of the sights of thousands of happy people, most with tears in their eyes. Half of the people did everything possible to welcome us home and the other half on the ship were expressing their gratitude for coming home. All of the wounded were removed first into hundreds of ambulances and buses. By mid-afternoon it was my turn to walk down the gangplank and step onto the good old U.S.A.

The Air Force had several buses waiting for us and we were driven over to New Jersey to Fort Lee. We spent several weeks at this base in order to get all of our papers processed, to have physicals, and to just simply play the Army game of "hurry up and wait." All of our meals were served in a mess hall, completely staffed by German Prisoners of War. This was another interesting experience. They were so damn efficient it was startling. I got a chance to get into New York City on several occasions; and yes, my first big meal was Maine lobster. I also got a free pass to see the New York play, "Bloomer Girl." I was given a box seat that actually protruded over the stage. Several times during the performance, I was embarrassed by some pretty singer directing her song right at me, much to the audience's amusement. Finally, I was given my orders, a 60-day leave of absence, and train tickets to my home in Wausau, Wisconsin, and another set of tickets to Ellington Field at Houston, Texas.

The train ride from New York Grand Central Station to Chicago Union Station seemed to take forever. I arrived in Chicago early in the morning so I had a whole day to kill. On Monday evening, October 9th I finally boarded the Hiawatha Train for the last leg of my trip up North.

172 • Returning Home

I sat up all night with the Porter, conversing while he shined shoes in the smoker. Waiting has never been one of my great virtues, and this night was no exception.

About 7:25 A.M., we gradually pulled to a stop in Rothschild, Wisconsin, a small town just south of Wausau, where I had previously informed the conductor that I preferred to get off. Once the train had stopped, the porter lifted my large duffel bag over one shoulder and grabbed my B-4 loaded bag with his last free arm and proceeded to fall down the steps onto the ground. The following scene I shall never forget. My future wife was racing toward me with outstretched arms, and my parents and future in-laws were all grouped together watching. I was bent over the porter trying to untangle him from all of my bags and hundreds of noses in the train were pressed up against the windows to watch this emotional return. It seems the Porter had passed the word along that this lucky returning veteran was coming home from the war to get married.

I'm glad it all happened just that way.

 Far Away Places

On Sunday morning, April 7, 1945, I received the news from the Base that I was a part of a group of eight crews that would ferry some attack bombers to Europe. These were two-men crews made up of a pilot and a navigator. We were going to Europe via South America and Africa, and the trip would take several weeks. I was informed that the pilot that I would be paired with was a Captain Greg Hillman, whom I'd never met. Our orders emphasized that we were to report to the Base prior to 0700 hrs. and to be ready to move out.

Since my return from combat, my new assignment was in the A.T.C. (Air Transport Command). Our primary function was to ferry airplanes and or supplies all over the world to our and allied forces. My base of operation for the ATC was at Rosecrans Field, St. Joseph, Missouri, a city of about 75,000 people in the northwest corner of the state. The work I was now doing was interesting because every other week I was in some different part of the world. When I returned from one of these trips, I had a minimum of three days off to spend with Norma, my wife of only a few months. I guess that my only regret with my new duties was that I could not have Norma by my side to share the wonderful sights.

This current assignment was going to be especially interesting and perhaps the main reason for relating the details herein. The additional instructions that I received were that we were being bused from Rosecrans Field at 0745 hrs. to Kansas City International Airport. We would then board a Delta Airline Flight that would take our group of 16 to Savannah, Georgia. I never knew why, but for some reason each of the flight crews were given vouchers for commercial flights with a number 2 priority. This high priority meant that when we checked in at the airport terminal for a flight, we were given 1st class seats on the very next flight out. On several occasions, I boarded planes that were already in take-off position and were called back to the terminal. On these flights where the plane taxied back, businessmen would have to leave the planes to give up seats for ATC crew members. In every case, we played out the old Army Game of Hurry Up and Wait.

173

174 • Far Away Places

On Monday I had to leave our apartment and Norma especially early in order to get out to the Base and make the bus for K.C. I knew over half of the fellows making this trip; however, this was my first meeting with my pilot, Captain Hillman. He was from Camden, New Jersey, and extremely handsome. I only mention this because everyone made comments that they thought we were brothers or even twins. In our uniforms this likeness was even more exaggerated. Several guys came up to me when Greg and I were apart and started a conversation that made no sense to me. Later our wives got to see the two of us together and came to the same conclusion. God, I'm glad he was handsome.

Our flight from Kansas City to Savannah gave us all a chance to get better acquainted and it went rather fast. An additional hour was required to take us from the airport to Hunter Army Air Base. Once we were settled, we were briefed that our job was to ferry eight A-26 Attack Bombers to a field at Poligniano near Naples, Italy. We were all to take off at approximately 1000 hours on Wednesday, April 10th.

The type of plane that we were ferrying was a new plane to me, but Captain Hillman had been checked out in it, as had all of the other pilots. The plane had been hurried out of the design stage and into production. The A-26, referred to as the "Marauder," looked a great deal like the A-20 Havoc, except it was slightly larger and faster and carried more armament. The plane was being rushed to Italy to be ready for the final stage of the war in Europe. It was believed that as the war wound down, Hitler would make a last ditch stand in the Alps at his famous Berchtegaden Retreat near the Austrian border. We were briefed on the A-26. It was a low altitude, high performance, two engine attack bomber designed for specific targets. It had no provision for oxygen, which meant that it would operate below 10,000 ft.

Since we had nearly all of Tuesday off and could do what we wanted, Greg and I went into Savannah and did some sight-seeing. At a remote corner of the city, we stumble onto a run down little shop that sold liquor. We stopped in to buy a bottle of anything worth drinking for the upcoming trip, but to our amazement the proprietor had two cases of straight bourbon whiskey. This type of drink was next to impossible to find during the war. Within minutes 24 bottles of "OLD MILL FARM" belonged to the twins. This stuff could be sipped right from the bottle and one could truly feel as it dribbled down your throat that this was the "nectar of the gods." The next morning we had to sneak this cargo of liquid gold onto our plane in order to get it back to St. Joe. What a trip coming up for so precious a cargo.

It was decided by the entire group that our ship would be the Lead Plane on this trip, primarily for two reasons. First, I was a lead navigator in combat in all but nine of my 35 missions; therefore, I had the most experience. Many navigators in this contingent served in the CBI Theater and some saw only limited duty. Secondly, Captain Hillman was the highest ranking officer. A few minutes after 1000 hours on Wednesday, we were all lined up and took off at one minute intervals. It had been decided that it would be less stressful if we didn't fly in formation, but rather as a loose group with radio contact maintained. This decision turned out to be a very important one on our third leg of this long journey.

The feeling in the cockpit of this A-26 was one of being crowded. On each side of us were engines the size of large automobiles that denoted raw power. The entire nose immediately in front of us was filled with guns and ammunition.

We were told at this briefing that it was next to impossible to bail-out from the plane because of the location of the engines and the high stabilizer. If we had to ditch this plane, we could expect it to sink in less than eight seconds. These were sobering statistics, especially since we were flying this brand new prototype that was manufactured by the lowest bidder.

The first leg of our trip was approximately 1,300 miles to Boringuen, Puerto Rico. Nearly all the legs on this journey would be 1,300 miles or slightly longer. On this clear day though, we would be able to see a continuous string of islands off our starboard side, making navigation very easy. About a half hour after taking off, we could see the skyline of Miami, Florida, in the distance off our right wing. About this time, I was fooling with the radio to pick up some music. Suddenly, the cockpit was filled with the sounds of Morse Code being tapped out. Our first thought that this might be someone in distress caught our immediate attention. I had a pad of paper strapped to my right knee so I immediately started to take this code down. As a navigator I had been exposed to this code at school, and we had to reach a moderate scale of proficiency before we graduated. That was long ago. Occasionally I would miss a letter but I was catching enough to spell out the word: " da dit da, dit da, dit da da dit, da, dit da, dit dit, da dit,— da da, dit dit, da dit dit, da dit, dit dit, da da dit, dit dit dit dit, da." Just as I was beginning to write down these letters CAPTAIN MIDNIGHT, a voice shouted out. "Captain Midnight." It was an old radio program for children. For the next several minutes, I had a feeling of a lot of room in my seat—I felt about 2" tall. During the course of this trip, Capt. Hillman made a point to tell this story to anyone who would listen.

Once we landed at the Base after our completion of the first leg of this journey, we checked into the bar of the Officers Club. A native Puerto Rican was the bartender and he could make one mean Old Fashion. We told him of our treasure that we found in Savannah so he proceeded to divulge his formula for putting this precious liquid to the best use. I think it important enough to include it here and now:

BORINGUEN OLD FASHION

1/2 lump sugar
2 dashes of Angostura Bitters
2 dashes of water to cover sugar
muddle well w/ right hand
1 medium size ice cube
2 oz. of OLD MILL FARM bourbon whiskey
Stir in clockwise direction w/ pinky
of right hand protruding.

Add twist of lemon rind and gently
drop into glass.
Decorate w/ slice of orange and 1/2 slice
of lemon and carefully place one cherry
in center.
Serve w/ stirring rod...sit back and
ENJOY.

Greg and I also had a chance to buy and to split a case of the best (as per our new found friend the Bartender) Puerto Rican Rum. With the addition of these six rum bottles, each of our B-4 bags, besides being heavy, were developing a shape for which they hadn't been designed.

On Thursday we took off on the next leg of our trip to a field just south of Georgetown, British Guiana. Georgetown is right on the Atlantic Ocean but we never left the Base to enjoy the sight. That evening Greg and I opened up several bottles of our bourbon and treated the others while we sat around just jawing. Little did any of us know that soon four of our number would be gone. Midway into the evening, we were all startled to learn that President Franklin D. Roosevelt had just died at Warm Springs, Georgia. We, of course, were saddened to learn this news. It took some time before any of us could remember who was vice president. Between the drinks that we had consumed and the fact that this was Roosevelt's fourth V.P. didn't help matters. We finally figured out that it was Harry Truman and all agreed that this tragedy would not change our role in the ongoing war. Oh yes, Greg and I had the fantastic opportunity to purchase a case of exquisite Dark Rum, which we also split. We had to throw away some articles of clothing and shoes to make room for our excellent gold. T-shirts and shorts were used to wrap each bottle to protect this treasure.

The third leg of our journey was going to be entirely over jungle. We were issued linen maps of the area. These maps showed little more than rivers and streams, since there were no cities, towns, or even villages indicated. They told us that these maps would hold up better in wet conditions. This was followed by the information that we could expect hordes of insects from thousand of species, snakes of all sizes, and natives who had never seen white-men, many of which practiced cannibalism. All of this information, along with the knowledge that I could not safely bail out of the damn plane, made me want to turn in their old map and my parachute.

The weather on this day was marginal when we took off, but it soon turned into lousy. We had to go approximately 1,000 miles to Bele'm, Brazil, and operations felt we would not have a problem. As we approached the halfway point, the ceiling dropped to within 100 feet of the tree tops. Sometimes there was less than 50 feet between the clouds that towered up to 12,000 ft. and the jungle growth. Occasionally, we had to lift up into the clouds to avoid especially high trees. Just before we reached the far border of French Guiana, one of the crews flying behind us yelled over the radio that two of our planes had crashed into the jungle. We circled back to see if there might be any signs of them and immediately ascertained that it would be impossible to help, let alone find where they went in. It is important to know that these jungle trees were several hundred feet tall and they made a complete umbrella over the floor of this foreign environment. The visibility was down to only one-half mile, and it was dangerous for six fast moving planes to be moving about under these conditions. We all agreed to head for Bele'm.

About 200 miles northeast of the field at Bele'm, the weather started to improve and we could see the Amazon River. The delta of the Amazon was right on our course and was over one hundred miles wide. It was an unbelievable sight—the world's greatest river dumping all its silt prior to entering the Atlantic Ocean. Another 100 miles and we could spot the field just north of town on the Tocantins River. Bele'm is really on the Bay de Marajo.

Because of the tragedy of the four killed airmen, we were given a day off to relax. Several of the fellows took this pretty hard. It was their first experience of being so close to death and having a friend have his number called. I don't know that you ever get used to this but my experience of combat over Germany had somehow steeled me not to dwell on these moments. My strong fatalistic attitude led me to believe that when your number was up it was time to cash in your chips—you had no choice.

During the day, I almost made the mistake of wandering too far down a path that led into the jungle. As the path ended, I took several additional steps into the maze of vegetation and discovered that I immediately lost all sense of direction. The jungle sounds, the heat and moisture, the insects, and most importantly the fear made me retrace my steps and get the hell out. The next morning at briefing I got the chance to see a boa constrictor that had been mounted in the office building. It was over 20 feet long and perhaps seven inches in diameter. It had swallowed a whole pig; that is how they caught it. This place was also on the equator so the sun was directly over your head and extremely hot. I would be happy to move on.

On Monday morning, the 15th of April, we headed for Natal, Brazil, about 1,100 miles away. This was our last stop before crossing the wide Atlantic. The only notable thing that I can recall about Natal was their extensive PX on the Base. I bought my wife Norma 12 pairs of silk stockings (these were not obtainable in the States) of various sizes, since I neglected to make note of the measurements of my new wife. I also purchased an alligator purse and a large bottle of Chanel No. 5 perfume. I found out later, when I arrived back at St. Joseph, Missouri, that all of the perfume evaporated at altitude because of the rare air. I did not know that I should have had the bottle sealed with wax to prevent this from happening. Nearly all of the silk stockings were not the right size, and I was informed that the alligator purse required a more extensive wardrobe than Norma possessed at the time. Oh well.

The next leg of this interesting experience was to fly from Natal to Asension Island, which was midway between South America and Africa. Our target was a small volcanic island, just large enough to have a single runway carved into it. This small protrusion in the Atlantic Ocean was about 1,500 miles away, our longest leg to date. This was a navigational challenge since a 1° error in course direction meant that we would be over 25 miles off course when we reached our destination. Ascension Island was a mere dot on any map, but it also proved to be a welcome sight once you spotted it. On this flight five or six new crews that were on their way to combat asked if they could tag along. During the flight I was in constant touch with the navigators so I could work with them to figure out headings; ETA's for let down and for arrival; wind direction by observing the relationship of their plane's altitude with the waves on the water surface; and the course we were flying. I did this same type of work with the navigators on the next day's leg.

The take-off from the relatively short runway was a little hairy on the morning of the 16th. This time, instead of a small dot in front of us, we had the entire Continent of Africa due east. Our destination was an airfield just north of Dakar, Senegal. An interesting surprise at this place was the mess hall. We were served by the nicest black waiters I had ever seen; they spoke perfect English with a British accent and possessed a bubbling personality. I truly enjoyed talking with each one that I was fortunate enough to meet.

Our trip today, April 18th, was partially over desert. This day was also my most memorable. After hours of flying over the desert with our wingtips hardly visible because of the haze, the last part of the trip to Marrakech, Morocco, was through the Atlas Mountains Range. We flew up a particular valley until a signal was received from a radio beacon, and then we altered our course at a prescribed time interval and took on a new heading down another canyon. This procedure was necessary because of the constant haze caused by the dust and sand particles in the air. Unknown to Greg and me, the radio beacon was not functioning. The Base at Dakar had mistakenly let us take-off while they stopped all other flights until repairs could be made. We were flying down a canyon, big dumb and happy, not knowing that our lives were in jeopardy. At the point when I had calculated that we should get needle action on our radio compass that should swing 180°, everything suddenly got dark in the cockpit. Captain Hillman pulled the controls down into his lap and nosed the A-26 toward the heavens. We climbed above the mountain peaks and into clearer air and swung the plane to the west and to the ocean. The dark effect that came into view was actually the shear walls of rock. We were inches away from certain death.

A short trip down the coast and then East over relatively flat land brought us to the airfield just East of Marrakakech. The Base was shocked that we had slipped through the precautions. This was as close as I'd ever come to cracking up in two years of flying and the several hundred thousand miles I had logged.

The flying from Morocco to Tunis in Tunisa was only about 1,200 miles. It was mostly over mountains and hilly country, and it had signs of being more fertile than anything that we had seen for the past few days. About an hour before we reached the Base at Tunis, we could see Algiers to the north of our course. The Base at Tunis was too far south to see the Mediterranean. We would have to wait for tomorrow's flight.

For some unknown reason, they did not schedule us to take off until late in the day. Of course, this was our shortest flight of the whole trip. It was only 400 miles north to Naples, Italy. When we were finally cleared for take-off, in all of the confusion and our desire to get out of there, Hillman and I both realized that a switch that had to be activated on the outside of the plane had been entirely forgotten. It was for IFF, a device that sends out a signal that receiving equipment will recognize a plane as friend or foe.

Because of the error and the time, we decided to fly on the deck, just skimming over the water so that radar would not pick us up. We were so low that occasionally we had to pull up to avoid hitting some small fishing boats. Some of them may have gotten swamped by our prop wash. It was dark as we approached Naples, and we still had to find an airfield at Poligniano, northeast of Naples. After some difficulty with a British control tower operator, who we could hardly understand, we finally touched down. Because no one seemed to be alert, we could have blown up the whole place, if we had been an enemy. By the time we checked in the delivery of this new or almost new, A-26, we got our heavy B-4 bags with over 20 bottles of fluid off the plane; we were ready for the bed they pointed out to us.

We had a free day on Sunday so we got transportation into Naples. This was a very disappointing experience for me. In all of my reading and studying architectural buildings, I had been led to believe that this was one of Europe's most beautiful cities. It turned out to be a disaster for me. My impressions have completely destroyed any desire of ever returning. Though the war had gone through this city over a year ago, I could see battle damage and all of the debris laying everywhere. No one had made an effort to clean up anything. While I was in England for my tour of combat duty, I witnessed whole blocks and neighborhoods being destroyed. By the next morning, the British would have the streets passable for vehicles; and in a day or two, the rubble was picked up and put into the hold of ships for ballast and was being sent to the USA for removal. Everywhere I walked in Naples, I noticed that the fronts of buildings had been blown out, and I could see people on each floor living with little or no regard for privacy. No effort was made to even keep the elements out. The most disappointing experience, however, was the many times that I was approached by men who were selling the sexual services of their wives or daughters. To this day, I find this hard to live with.

On Monday morning we boarded an Air Force C54 Transport Plane for the long flight to Casablanca, Morocco. On this trip we could sit back and leave the flying to others. We were informed that there would be a several day delay due to a backlog of people returning to the United States. Once we settled in on the Base at Casablanca, we were given the bad news that all ATC Personal would be put on a standby list to ferry war weary planes back to the States. The last one on this waiting list would be required to serve on ferry crews. I had seen several old B-17s at one end of the field so I immediately thought my destiny was sealed. My first thought was that perhaps I could bribe my way off one of these flights by giving up several bottles of my liquor. The distasteful part of sticking

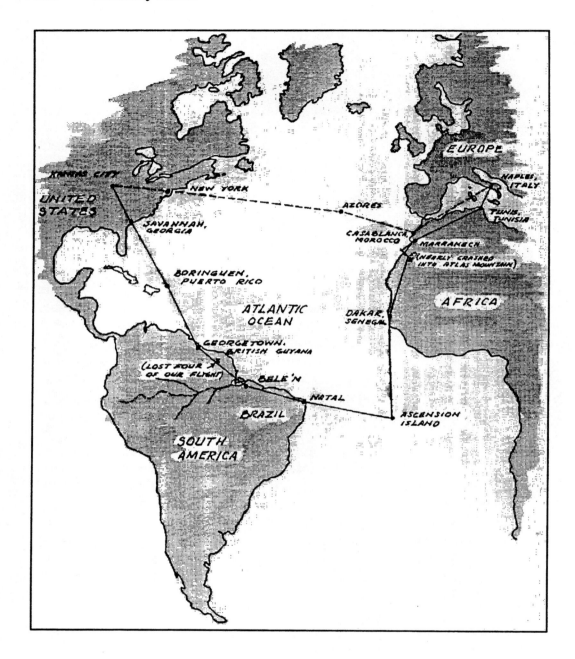

my neck out for returning war weary planes was that once they were delivered, they would be destroyed. I had lost several friends in the ATC from such operations. My worries were all for nothing because a large group of other ATC crews blew in and I was moved way up the standby list.

I spent five days in Casablanca before I was scheduled to fly out by Military Transport on April 27th. I searched for Rick's Place but was never able to locate it. I did have one scare though, when a small group of Arab kids were supposedly taking us to a specific place. Greg and I noticed that as this group of kids kept growing in number that we were also being led down narrower streets into a rough looking area. On a given signal, we both slammed our way through these kids and ran like hell. We both felt that we were about to get rolled.

We took off shortly after 1,200 hours on a beautiful Saturday morning. Our first stop was in the Azores, a group of islands about a 1,000 miles west of Portugal and Spain. We spent a few hours off the plane to eat while the plane was being refueled. The entire group of military passengers again boarded this C-54 for the longer leg on the trip to New York.

The flight to New York was long and took most of the night. I was able to get some much needed rest. The positive thing that helped me mentally was the fact that we were crossing time zones and this was moving our watches back. Early Sunday morning on the 28th of April, we landed at La Guardia International Airport in New York City. My first surprise was going through customs. Yep, you guessed it. My B-4 bag immediately caught the eye of this custom official. The first clue was its weight and the second clue was the noise it made when I sat it down on the inspection counter. I was informed that the law stated that I could only enter the country with 4 quarts or 5 fifths of alcohol. It was a good thing that I was ignorant of this; otherwise, I wouldn't have tried something so ridiculous. The custom official was really swell about the whole matter. First, he offered to take me home for supper if I would bring a bottle of the bourbon along. I told him that I had a No. 2 flight priority pass and was expected to return immediately to our ATC Base at Rosecrans Field. I stated that I had been gone nearly three weeks, an unusually long time for plane delivery. I stated that my pilot had been back at our Base for over three days already and they would be expecting me. I offered him a bottle, but he told me that he couldn't accept. He immediately winked and gave me permission to pass through. His last word was "enjoy". The fact that I was a decorated war veteran didn't hurt a ridiculous cause. God, this booze had a lot of miles on it.

It only took me two hours to get booked on a commercial flight back to Kansas City. Once again, I was racing with the sun and the hour hand was moving favorably. A call to the Base got me transportation back to St. Joseph and Norma. We sat up until the wee hours of the morning while I tried to relate the many things written here.

The trip covered a great distance and touched many countries. I could see just how large our world was and also how small it was growing. I had the opportunity to see different peoples and different cultures. I flew over oceans, jungles, deserts, and mountains to deliver a single airplane, whose sole function (getting Hitler out of the Alps) was never realized.

The A-26 Marauder was a fine plane that never really got a chance to prove itself because of the pending end of the long and terrible war. Jets were soon to take over flight. However, I shall always have fond memories of the hours that I sat in this plane's cockpit, and I will always be grateful for how it functioned.

After several days rest, I once again returned to my Base and inquired where I was being sent next. Every corner of our globe is different and each has its own special interest. By the way, Norma thanked me for the pair of silk stockings, the beautiful glass bottle that had held Chanel #5, and the alligator purse that she felt some day she might find an outfit with which it would go. I just think she was glad to see me after my three week journey.

95TH BOMB GROUP REUNION

In May 1989, a reunion took place in Horham, England, home of the 95th Bomb Group. A special tour was organized in the States for 38 veterans and their wives to fly over to England. Norma and I were in Europe at the time and we organized our trip so that we could join the group for this special occasion.

The visit to the original field at Horham was both nostalgic and disappointing. The entire complex had all but disappeared, with only the main concrete runway remaining and a few scattered structures in complete disarray. The concrete perimeters and the hardstands had been torn up and the land put back into agriculture. One building, a structure that formerly housed the NCO Club, had the possibility of being restored. Some of our English friends felt it could be converted into a museum for the 95th and were making plans accordingly.

All Americans attending this reunion boarded buses for the ride over the Framlingham to visit the former 390th Bomb Group Parham airfield. The members of our brother group, along with British neighbors, had completely restored their control tower and had made it into their museum. Since all control towers appeared to be constructed from the same set of architectural drawings, it was not hard to visualize our own mission structure. The museum at the 390th contained USAF uniforms, decorations, combat records, special equipment collected from our former base, war photographs, and other memorabilia. This museum is run by volunteers in the area in honor of all members of the Eighth Air Force.

One of the most interesting moments of this reunion was the special service held in St. Mary's Church in Horham. The tiny village is located in Suffolk and is midway between Norwich and Ipswich. It dates back to the time of the Saxons, with evidence of its existence in the late 900s. The church, originally a wooden structure, was built a thousand years ago. It was rebuilt in stone by the Normans in the year 1086. This early structure is a part of the church that is still being used by its parishioners, who so graciously welcomed us. The pastor and the members of this congregation let each of us know that our efforts 45 years ago had not been forgotten. Their sincere gratitude left each of us with tears in our eyes.

During this memorial service, we all became aware of a unique problem that the people of this small village inherited. Nearly 60 years ago the bells of this very special church were silenced because the structural wooden framework had rotted and did not have sufficient strength to support the heavy bells. The congregation could not afford to replace the required superstructure and the other repair work necessary so that the oldest ring of eight bells in the world could once again be in operating condition. There were four bells in the tower in the year 1553, with a fifth bell cast in 1605. The other three bells were cast by the Ipswich Foundry of John Darbie between the years 1651 and 1693.

We (Air Force veterans) became aware that over the years the congregation had collected approximately $17,000 for the required work, while the cost for the necessary repairs was rising faster than the funds could be collected. Our entire reunion group volunteered to take up the challenge with the 95th Bomb Group Association. A plan, called "The Ring of Eight," was organized to restore these bells in remembrance of the many comrades who lost their lives flying from the Horham airfield. Over $30,000 was raised and sent to our friends from this small village.

The oldest remaining octave of bells in the world has now been restored. There will be a special dedication in May 1992, with members of the 95th Bomb Group and the people of Horham taking part on this auspicious occasion. Some of these bells were last tolled in 1933, but the last full peal was rung in 1911.

I talked with one very interesting lady who was a small girl when the Americans were taking off on missions. She had kept a diary of how many planes lumbered down the long runway and took to the air with a full load of bombs. She could hear the sounds of the laboring aircraft engines in her upstairs bedroom in the early hours of the morning. When she returned from school, she again listened for the returning planes. Even as a child, she knew that if the count did not add up, that many airmen had met with trouble. Many of these English families had sons of their own who were serving in some remote spot in world. They treated the Americans as they hoped others would accept their men.

Most of the people we talked to were small children who had begged for candy and attention from the men of the 95th. "Any gum chum" was their favorite expression. Today, at this reunion, they appeared to be about the same age as all of the returning veterans, with the usual amount of gray hair. It was easy to forget that we were practically children when we served our country. Six or seven years difference in age does not seem like a lot once you get in your 70s.

On May 6, 1989, during a noon luncheon with our friends from the Horham area, Roger Freeman welcomed everyone to the 95th Bomb Group Reunion. I believe his remarks at this occasion sum up how the people of the Suffolk area in England felt about the "Bloody Yanks." Roger Freeman is considered the foremost authority on the history of the Eighth Air Force during World War II. The following is the complete text of Roger's remarks:

"As a young schoolboy in 1943, I visited the airfield at Horham on several occasions and I saw the SQUARE B Fortresses of the 95th Bomb Group. You were young men in a strange land, complaining that the beer in the pubs was always weak and too warm. And you wondered if, and when, it was ever going to stop raining.

All that was a long time ago. The old world has taken several whirls since then, but here we are. . . . our youth is gone, we are all getting a bit snowy on top; some of us have nothing on top at all and our old bodies aren't what they were. They stick in where they should stick out, and they stick out where they should stick in. But don't worry, because I might have been just a kid then, but I'm also sliding past middle age just like you gentlemen. And as I said, it's a long time ago; and since then there have been many, many changes.

You have all been just down the road to see some other changes at your old airfield. It's not the Horham base that you remember of nearly 50 years ago. You say to yourselves: 'Is this really the place where there were 150,000 takeoffs and landings? Is this the place where we sent nearly 20,000 tons of bombs to Adolf Hitler and his cronies? Is this the place where the B-17s of the old SQUARE B took off at dawn from that runway which was the highway to battlefields far away? Is this the place where we sweated in a machine shop, or where we froze on a cold winter day out on the airfield as we tried to change the spark plugs on a Wright Cyclone engine? Is this the place where we spent long and sleepless nights in those tin can Nissen Huts while hearing the mechanics out on the field winding up our B-17 engines in preparation for tomorrow's mission? Is this the place from where the Fortresses of the 95th set off for the first daylight raid over Berlin? Is this the place where the gunners of the 95th were credited with more enemy aircraft destroyed than any other outfit in the 8th Air Force Bomber Command? Is this really the place where we spent our youth—perhaps two days—perhaps two years?

Horham is the same place, and as everything else, it changes. But there is one thing that hasn't changed; and that is the feeling of the people of Horham and Suffolk County for what you Americans did and what you were. That has not changed!

It may surprise you after half a century that you are even remembered. But you are, and you can see that you are. Why are you remembered? You have faith in what you did, and you have faith in what you are. You have faith in the 611 who left this airfield and never returned home. You have faith in the old SQUARE B.

We are an old nation, and appreciate people who have faith in the past and do not forget—because we don't forget either. Welcome back 95th and please come again."

Roger Freeman is the author of *The Mighty Eighth*, *The Mighty Eighth War Diary*, *Epics of Aviation Archaeology* and several other books.

Epilogue

If I had not returned to Horham, England, in Suffolk during the month of May 1989, I doubt that I would have had the inclination to relate my story during the historic days of World War II. For some unknown reason, my visit to the area from which the 95th Bomb Group operated from April 1943 to August 1945 triggered memories of my small contribution to the total effort.

I was one of the over two million Americans who answered the call to arms. My story has to be considered typical of the many young men who served in the Eighth Air Force. For over 45 years, I had put the war out of my mind and definitely behind me. After my discharge, I had new challenges such as being a husband, a father, a scholar, an architect, a cattle breeder, and an active citizen in my community.

Upon my return from the reunion with our English friends at Horham, I found that memories were resurrected from an "inner me" that I did not know existed. In the early hours of the morning of a sleepless night, my stories flowed as though they had happened only days before. My entire experience that I was reliving created an almost eery feeling, one in which each moment accurately fell into place in a proper sequence. The one big difference between now and then was that the parts came together with greater meaning. I could see reasons for things that I had just accepted while in combat. I could feel feelings that I had been immune to and I could once again sense the fear that I had learned to overcome. I am now aware of the gratitude I perhaps took for granted as a member of a combat crew. Now, I have the privilege, at the age of 71, to be able to record these moments of my life, knowing that over 49,000 of my flying brothers did not have this option.

The 95th Bomb Group lost 611 of its very best. I now believe that it is most important that this period of time be remembered by future generations as an America capable of putting forth its best effort for any cause worth resolving. There is much to be learned from the recording of the events of this period of time. Our country would do well to recapture the will and spirit of the forties.

I would be derelict if I did not mention the tremendous pride that I have of my 95th Bomb Group. It was the only Group in the entire Eighth Air Force awarded three Distinguished Unit Citations. It was the first American Group to bomb Berlin, Germany, during daylight. The date was March 4, 1944. During the period of operation, the 95th flew 321 missions and was credited with destroying 425 enemy aircraft, more than any 8th Air Force bomb group. An additional 117 planes were probably destroyed and 231 damaged. These were all credited to the 95th. Its B17's flew 8,903 sorties while dropping nearly 20,000 tons of bombs on enemy targets. I'm proud to have been a part of this particular group.

It is important for me to state my feelings toward the British people for whom I have strong affection. During the war I grew to respect their bravery and determination to withstand the continuous bombing and harassment from the German Air Force and the thousands of V-1 and V-2 missiles rained down upon them. Their will to fight back (over four years by themselves) was unequaled. I doubt that any other people could have withstood their ordeal with such valor, humor, and resolve.

When I returned to England in 1989 to visit my former base, I can truthfully say that I hardly had a dry eye during the two days of the reunion. My wife and I, as well as other 95th members, were made to feel especially welcome and most assuredly made to realize that all of our sacrifices were appreciated. The sincerity of our former allies was perhaps the main reason that I was move to put my story on paper.

I have added a few other items that might prove interesting and are a small part of my story. The map of East Anglia indicated the location and to which Division each Group of the heavy bombers belonged. The concentration of the might of the Eighth Air Force, along with the many Fighter Groups, was located in only a small portion of England. The copy of the several envelopes are but a few of the hundreds of letters that I sent my fiance (presently my wife) during the war. The contents of the actual letters are not a part of this story.

Cover of program for the speical services held in
St. Mary's Church at Horham, England, 1989.

192 • Epilogue

This is the beautiful marble memorial dedicated in September, 1981. It reads as follows:
   "In memory of the men of the 95th Bombardment Group who served at Horham Airfield and to those who gave their lives in the cause of freedom.
1943-1945

* * *

334, 335, 336, 412 bomb squadrons and supporting units. Headquarters 13th Combat Bomb Wing, United States 8th Air Force."

Photo at 95th memorial.
Part of the group of 38 veterans who returned 45 years later, in May, 1989.
Marble memorial was placed on a dedicated piece of land in front of church. A large box "B" is carved on other face of tail section.

194 • Epilogue

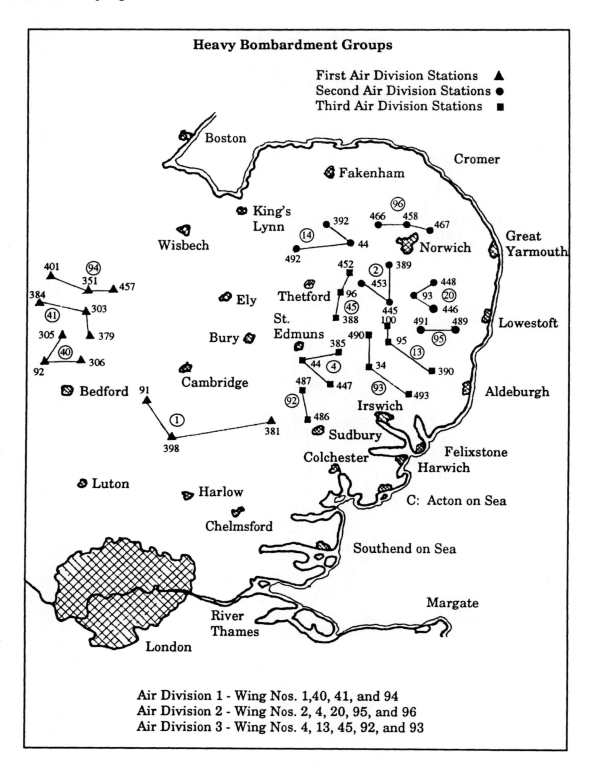

The following envelopes are typical of the many letters I mailed Norma. I wrote nearly every day and nearly every envelope had a cartoon on the front. Only have room here for six such experiences of I. M. Cocky.

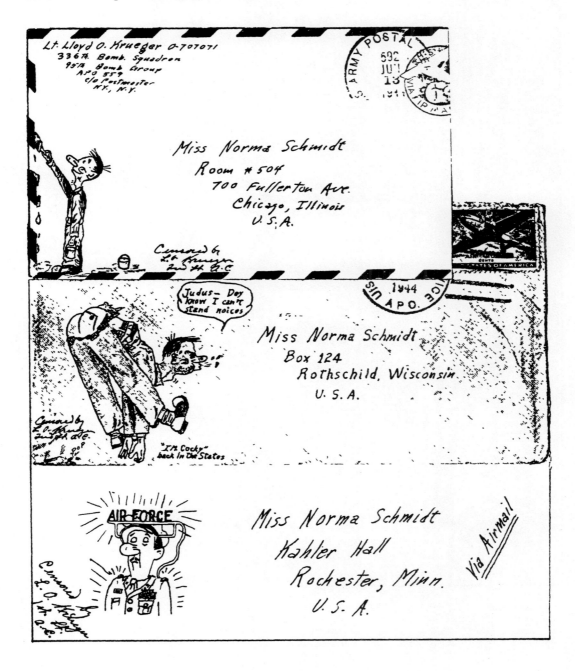

196 • Epilogue

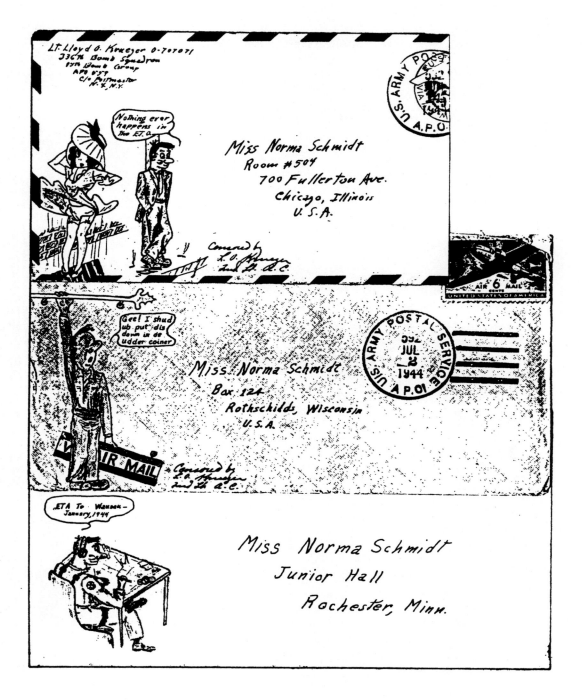

These three photographs were taken in England by photographer who tried to make us appear as an ordinary European. The purpose for these pictures, which I carried on my person on all missions, was to be able to turn them over to the underground should we be shot down. With proper photographs, they could rapidly forge passports, giving Americans a better chance to escape.

On August 27, 1944, the 95th Bomb Group flew its 200th mission. A big party was held in the hanger with Glen Miller and his orchestra providing the music. Shortly after this engagement Glen Miller was lost at sea while flying to France. Our group was to go on and fly a total of 321 missions before the war was over.

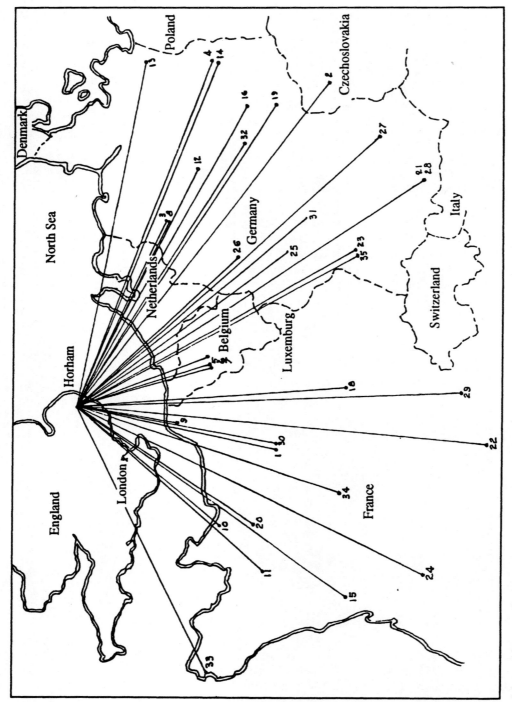

Map of Europe locating targets and missions I participated in. Number indicate credited missions with date and target listed on page 202.

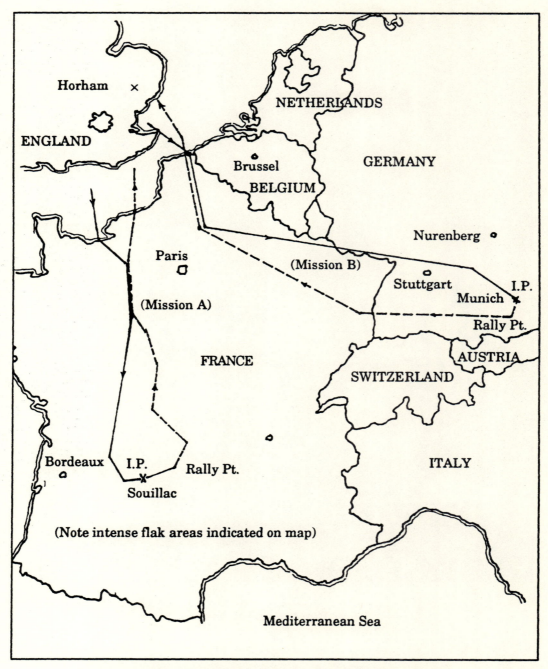

Partial Map of Europe Indicating Two Typical Missions
(See actual pilot maps on following pages)

MISSION A
Route Map to Souillac, France

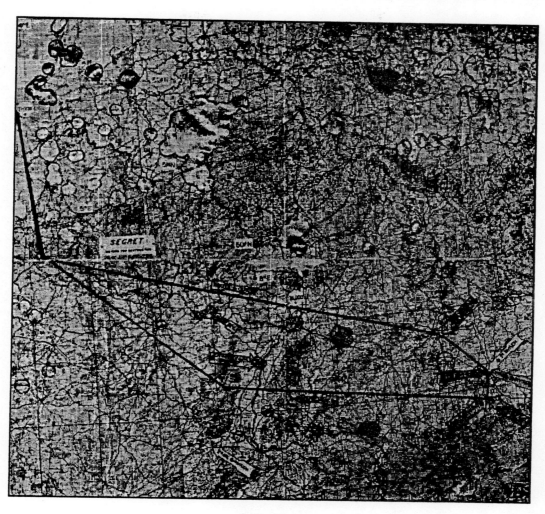

MISSION B
Route Map to Munich, Germany

LISTS OF MISSIONS FLOWN

Lt. Lloyd O. Krueger participated in the following missions as confirmed by the CO of the 95th Bomb Group (H):

No.	Date	Target
1	5-09-44	Laon Athies, France
2	5-12-44	Brux, Czechoslovakia
3	5-13-44	Osnabruck, Germany
4	5-19-44	Berlin, Germany
5	5-20-44	Brussels, Belgium
6	5-25-44	Brussels, Belgium
7	5-30-44	Brussels, Belgium
8	5-31-44	Osnabruck, Germany
9	6-05-44	Boulogne, France
10	6-06-44	Caen, France (D-Day)
11	6-12-44	Vitry-en-Arteis, France
12	6-15-44	Hannover, Germany
13	6-20-44	Fellersleben, Germany
14	6-21-44	Berlin, Germany (Basdorf)
15	6-24-44	Fruges, France
16	6-29-44	Leipzig, Germany (Bohlen)
17	7-04-44	Gein, France
18	7-06-44	Fiefs, France
19	7-07-44	Kolleda, Germany (Leipzig
20	7-08-44	Bernay, France
21	7-12-44	Munich, Germany (Munchen)
22	7-14-44	St. Medard, France (French Maquis)
23	7-16-44	Stuttgart, Germany
24	7-17-44	Cheny, France
25	7-18-44	Hemmingstedt, Germany
26	7-20-44	Lutkendorf, Germany (Halle)
27	7-21-44	Regensburg, Germany
28	7-31-44	Munich, Germany (Munchen)
29	8-01-44	Lac d'Anncey, France (French Maquis)
30	8-02-44	Invasion Front (Tactical Mission)
31	8-24-44	Ruhland, Germany
32	8-25-44	Muritz Lake, Germany (Politz)
33	8-26-44	Brest, France
34	9-03-44	Lanveoc, France
35	9-05-44	Stuttgart, Germany

ROLL OF HONOR

The following is a list of those assigned to the 95th Bombardment Group (H) who made the ultimate sacrifice to their country.

11-12-43	Abbadessa, Frank J.	21-02-44	Blanchard, Robert M.
13-06-43	Adams, William C.	06-11-44	Blazques, Vinvent
10-01-45	Adcock, Ernest L.	06-02-44	Bleyenberg, Francis C.
04-03-44	Aiello, Vincent	02-08-44	Bockman, Elmer E.
09-10-43	Allen, Grant E.	03-03-45	Bohlander, Chester F.
13-06-43	Alojado, Simon E.	18-06-44	Bordelos, Pierre L.
21-02-44	Amberg, George L.	11-06-44	Borden, Raymond C.
09-10-43	Anderson, James R.	11-04-44	Boren, J. W.
11-04-44	Andres, Oliver A.	10-02-44	Boswell, James R.
26-07-43	Angle, Ambros B.	13-06-43	Boyd, Odes W.
29-01-44	Archibald, Vern E.	19-07-44	Bradburn, Francis J.
21-05-43	Auld, Philip N.	unknown	Brady, Frederick W.
24-05-44	Averas, Gregory P.	20-12-43	Brass, Fred
02-08-44	Baber, Robert O.	25-07-43	Brick, Thomas B.
11-06-43	Babich, George	30-11-44	Briggs, Warren E.
25-07-43	Bachman, Edwin L.	25-08-44	Briley, Barton E.
11-04-44	Backowski, John J.	27-05-43	Briska, Frederick W.
26-07-43	Bail, David E.	13-06-43	Broch, Clayton E.
18-02-43	Baker, Gerald W.	06-04-45	Brooks, Jacob
27-05-43	Baldassaro, Frank A.	28-07-43	Brooks, Lloyd R.
06-04-45	Ballou, William O.	11-04-44	Brown, Louis J.
10-10-43	Balmer, Harry F.	13-06-43	Brown, Raymond L.
27-05-43	Banks, Stanley B.	28-09-44	Brown, Warren W.
11-04-44	Bannerman, Richard P.	28-07-43	Brown, William R.
12-02-44	Barbella, Vincent J.	13-06-43	Bruce, Charles S.
10-10-43	Baros, Lee	23-06-44	Bruniga, Eugene C.
21-02-44	Barron, Thomas P.	28-07-43	Brunson, William F.
04-03-44	Barstow, Clarence N.	30-11-44	Bryce, Gordon K.
27-07-43	Basties, Marion O.	24-05-44	Bubbett, Victor L.
09-10-43	Bates, Ralph T.	07-05-45	Bubolz, Edward N.
29-12-43	Baughman, Roy D.	29-01-44	Buchanan, Robert B.
16-12-44	Beadle, Leonard W.	10-10-43	Buckley, William E.
06-03-44	Beal, Marion B.	07-10-44	Buds, Charles W.
24-05-44	Beck, Charles W.	10-07-43	Budnick, Leonard A.
10-01-45	Bell, Clyde R.	07-01-45	Bull, Milton F.
03-02-45	Bell, Marion L.	18-06-44	Bullard, Jonathon N.
20-01-45	Bennett, Delbert D.	13-06-43	Buller, Howard
11-06-43	Bennett, Stanley D.	09-10-43	Burdick, John C.
13-06-43	Benson, Charles J.	24-05-44	Burgman, Orin V.
29-05-43	Berntzen, Yngvar S.	06-02-44	Burgo, Augustine
23-03-45	Bitner, Clarence R.	06-02-44	Burke, Richard A.

28-07-43	Burliegh, Lawernce C.	26-07-43	Cothran, Charles B.
23-03-45	Burnett, Clarence J.	25-08-44	Covel, Orlin K.
24-01-43	Burris, C.J.	10-02-44	Cowdery, Donald A.
11-12-43	Byard, Robert J.	16-09-43	Cox, Dewey J.
11-01-44	Cadle, Warren S.	10-01-44	Coyle, Ralph W.
11-06-44	Cambell, Ellsworth L.	21-05-43	Craig, Charles T.
24-01-44	Canard, James F.	10-01-44	Croker, Michael D.
16-08-44	Cantrell, Eugene	23-03-45	Cullerne, Wilfred B.
27-05-43	Carlisle, John E.	12-08-44	Cullum, Marcus B.
17-08-43	Carlone, Anthony L.	13-06-43	Cummings, Burrill
07-01-45	Carlson, Carl L.	25-07-43	Cummins, Eldon J.
11-04-44	Carlson, Roland L.	11-04-44	Cunliffe, Edward T.
03-03-45	Carr, John C.	16-08-44	Curtis, James C.
25-07-43	Carr, Robert N.	21-02-44	Cuyler, Leroy M.
27-05-43	Caroll, Byron A.	02-08-44	Dallas, Raymond D.
14-06-44	Carter, Elvis L.	16-12-43	Darter, Eugene F.
25-07-43	Carter, George A.	17-10-44	Davies, NMI
11-04-44	Cartrite, Harvey L.	06-04-45	Davis, Robert L.
18-06-44	Casselman, Everett M.	11-06-43	Davorenm John F.
06-03-44	Cassidy, John N.	21-02-44	Decker, Delmar A.
13-11-43	Castons, E. J.	16-12-43	Delbern, Frederick A.
24-01-43	Cattros, L. A.	06-02.44	Denar, Domenick
11-06-43	Cavanaugh, Richard M.	21-02-44	Derenberg, Frank W.
13-06-43	Chambers, Kenneth C.	23-03-45	Detweiler, Raymond W.
26-07-43	Cisar, Joseph B.	12-08-43	Deverger, Claude E.
15-09-43	Clapper, Billie E.	11-04-44	Deyaeger, Raymond A.
29-05-43	Clark, Lawrence D.	26-07-43	Dickey, Volis E.
11-12-43	Claybaugh, Paul N.	19-11-43	Diete, Richard F.
13-06-43	Clinton, Ivan A.	16-08-44	Dixon, William N.
13-06-43	Clear, R. D.	26-07-43	Dodson, James M.
06-04-45	Coalson, John D.	16-12-43	Dodson, Loren E.
15-09-43	Cochras, William L.	29-12-43	Downey, Eugene
16-12-44	Coffman, Harold C.	13-06-43	Drost, Stephen
31-12-44	Cobea, Charles	13-06-43	Drotleff, Walter P.
10-02-44	Cole, Charles F.	03-03-45	Duncan, Robert L.
20-12-43	Comps, Neil A.	13-06-43	Dunn, Rheaums E.
13-06-43	Conklin, Lester	24-01-44	Durkin, Thomas L.
20-01-45	Conover, Aaron C.	11-12-43	Eaton, Leonard W.
21-02-44	Cook, Harold E.	14-06-44	Edwards, Lunsford C.
13-11-43	Cook, James J.	09-10-43	Eherts, Ralph W.
07-05-45	Cook, Russel N.	27-05-43	Eliak, Sam P.
13-06-43	Copeland, Victor T.	10-04-44	Enstrom, Everett T.
10-10-43	Cornell, Joseph P.	29-01-44	Esala, Larry R.
13-06-43	Corsett, Owen W.	10-01-45	Eerett, Elbert V.
12-08-44	Corrigan, Walter L.	31-12-44	Exley, Walter A.
19-11-43	Cosley, Kenneth	15-09-43	Fabritz, Daniel J.

23-03-45	Facteau, Paul L.	10-02-44	Hardeman, Jackson O.
06-04-45	Fascenelli, Albert	13-06-43	Hardy, Robert W.
28-07-43	Fear, Merle C.	18-04-44	Hargraves, Elbert E.
14-06-44	Feiler, Reuben T.	10-07-43	Harmon, Edwin M.
13-06-43	Finch, Lawrence	03-03-45	Harvey, Thomas J.
31-12-44	Finklestein, Herman	06-03-44	Hazlett, David W.
27-05-43	Finn, Albert E.	31-12-44	Heafey, Morgan J.
21-02-44	Flowers, Charlie N.	25-07-43	Healey, John J.
13-06-43	Foley, Albert J.	11-12-43	Healey, Malcolm O.
13-06-43	Forest, Robert L.	13-06-43	Healey, Thomas F.
13-06-43	Forrest, Nathan B.	19-07-44	Heil, James A.
26-07-43	Foutz, Stanley	11-04-44	Henderson, Roy E.
11-04-44	Francis, Leo C.	27-05-43	Henderson, Wallace E.
13-06-43	Francis, Robert F.	07-10-44	Hendrian, Robert A.
26-07-43	Franklin, Marthal N.	24-05-44	Hentz, Jerome J.
06-03-44	Frantz, Charles M.	18-06-44	Hertes, Austin N.
06-03-44	Freyer, Charles N.	29-01-44	Higgins, James D.
07-10-44	Fromas, Donald W.	07-10-44	Higgins, Robert C.
14-06-44	Fuller, Kirby	17-08-43	Hill, Charles E.
29-12-43	Gaffney, William J.	02-08-44	Hill, Robert V.
29-01-44	Gallagher, Don A.	07-10-44	Hillgardner, Albert L.
16-12-44	Gallagher, Edward W.	14-05-43	Hilliard, John R.
12-08-43	Gardner, Clee N.	21-02-44	Hines, Rodney D.
06-02-44	Gaudet, Allen J.	26-07-43	Hock, Donald C.
13-06-43	Gay, Frederick C.	28-07-43	Hodges, Fred D.
06-03-44	Giddens, Daniel R.	30-07-43	Hollerman, Robert C.
18-06-44	Gioioss, John E.	18-06-44	Holmes, William
27-05-43	Gira, John F.	18-02-43	Hooberry, Charles R.
11-04-44	Gopigian, Thomas	16-12-44	Hooser, William E.
11-12-43	Goss, David E.	13-06-43	Hoover, Floyd C.
29-12-43	Grant, Alan S.	21-01-44	Hudson, William A.
07-01-45	Gree, Frank J.	23-06-44	Huff, Albert S.
30-11-44	Gresman, Herchel R.	13-06-43	Hughes, Noah T.
21-02-44	Griffen, Howard L.	13-06-43	Huges, Tink J.
28-07-43	Grody, William N.	12-08-44	Humms, Val F.
28-07-43	Guenther, Warren W.	29-01-44	Humphrey, Robert P.
29-11-43	Guinzburg, Ralph V.	04-03-44	Hurley, John
06-04-45	Gunaard, Frederick T.	24-01-44	Inman, John
13-06-43	Guse, William C.	27-05-43	Irwin, Harry
31-03-44	Gussett, James W.	12-07-44	Iverson, Lloyd M.
13-06-43	Hale, Roderick W.	15-03-44	Jaceles, Theodore
06-02-44	Hamby, Leo C.	10-02-44	Jackson, William
12-08-43	Hamilton, Clifford B.	11-04-44	Janofsky, David
20-12-43	Hamilton, Richard C.	18-06-44	Jarrett, Lorenze
16-08-44	Hannun, Allen E.	26-07-43	Jenkins, Elden F.
03-02-45	Hansen, Leroy N.	13-06-43	Jennings, Robert M.

11-04-44	Jerstad, Edward M.	20-03-45	Larnard, William A.
17-07-43	Jesiolowski, Edward A.	13-06-43	Lawton, Edward A.
11-04-44	Jett, Paul E.	29-12-43	Leddy, Howard J.
13-06-43	Johnson, Charles D.	29-12-43	Leithhead, James W.
30-11-44	Johnson, Fred D.	03-03-45	Lelly, Courtney U.
25-07-43	Johnson, John W.	22-12-43	Lembeka, Donald F.
16-12-44	Jones, John J.	27-05-43	Lewis, Clinton L.
11-04-44	Jones, John P.	13-06-43	Lewis, Edwin R.
30-07-43	Jordon, Harold W.	26-07-43	Lewis, Ivan C.
13-06-43	Julliard, Louis J.	11-04-44	Ligoe, William H.
16-08-44	Karpe, Leland E.	11-04-44	Lillo, Wallace C.
02-08-44	Kayler, Jasper W.	18-03-44	Lintelman, Joseph D.
13-06-43	Kearsey, Grady V.	31-03-44	Lipchitz, Max R.
04-08.44	Keck, Alphonso J.	13-06-43	Locke, Floyd A.
17-10-44	Kehoe, William J.	16-08-44	Loehwing, Kenneth N.
05-01-44	Kelleher, James J.	07-10-44	Loftis, William D.
unknown	Keller, John J.	28-07-43	Lofton, Harold B.
20-12-43	Kelley, William P.	30-11-43	Lohmane, William L.
10-10-43	Kelly, Joseph R.	29-12-43	Loija, Raymond A.
24-01-43	Kelly, Norval W.	12-07-44	Loughner, Russell R.
03-03-45	Kelody, Rudolph W.	29-01-44	Lugg, John E.
06-04-45	Kennedy, Dale J.	10-07-43	Luttrell, John A.
22-06-44	Kent, Norris J.	12-08-44	Lyon, Charles R.
10-02-44	Kerestes, Henry M.	24-04-43	MacDonald, C. D .
25-08-44	Kieinman, Lawrence	13-06-43	MacDonald, William M.
29-01-44	Kiner, William F.	13-06-43	MacIntosh, Gordon E.
22-06-43	King, Harold T.	11-06-43	MacKinnon, Malcolm B.
07-01-45	Klein, Oscar B.	26-07-43	MacNeil, John L.
11-12-43	Klemp, Arthur E.	12-08-44	Madigan, John F.
10-02-44	Knox, William E.	06-03-44	Mailman, Albert J.
20-01-45	Kodish, Allen B.	10-04-44	Manahan, Blaine R.
unknown	Korber, John J.	23-06-44	Mangan, Daniel J.
07-05-45	Korber, Robert W.	22-12-43	Mangis, Maurice W.
11-04-44	Kress, Henry S.	11-06-43	Mareck, Alexander A.
11-06-44	Kuchung, Ewalt E.	21-02-44	Marks, Morris R.
16-08-44	Kuns, Richard F.	31-12-44	Maraik, Anthony A.
07-05-45	Kuper, Gerald I.	02-11-44	Martin, James E.
30-11-44	Kurz, Nelson F.	10-01-45	Mason, George W.
29-01-44	Kvickstrom, Ragnar A.	13-06-43	Mason, Kenneth C.
13-06-43	LaSarge, Joseph L.	26-07-43	Massey, Leroy A.
15-09-43	Lajois, Egar A.	16-08-44	Mathews, Fred C.
13-06-43	Lambert, John J.	18-02-43	Mattice, Norman K.
07-05-45	Lane, Gerald	25-07-43	Mauldin, Lloyd L.
07 05-45	Langford, William R.	14-06-44	Maylon, John E.
16-12-44	Lanni, Donald J.	13-06-43	Maylor ,William G.
20-01-45	Larkin, Edward D.	29-05-43	Mayo, Chester J.

21-02-44	McClellan, Lester W.	11-04-44	Murray, Ralph C.
20-12-43	McGonagle, Edward	13-06-43	Myers, Edward A.
21-02-44	McGuigan, John P.	14-06-44	Naylon, John E.
13-06-43	McInnis, Daniel H.	11-06-43	Neely, Windell D.
10-02-44	McKenna, Frank D.	16-12-43	Neff, Don P.
03-03-45	McKernan, Elbert R.	09-10-43	Nelson, John G.
14-05-43	McKinley, James E.	12-08-44	Newman, Paul F.
24-01-44	McLean, Douglas A.	28-07-43	Nix, Thomas J.
22-12-43	McMaster, William H.	15-09-43	Noyes, Joseph H.
10-07-43	McMullin, Donald S.	13-06-43	Nunes, Joseph L.
13-06-43	McMurtry, Glenn W.	26-09-43	O'Malley, John R.
13-06-43	McNeely, Cuceri J.	31-12-44	O'Reilly, Charles H.
11-04-44	McNeil, Donald J.	12-08-43	Ocheltree, Lydle C.
13-06-43	McNutt, Robert L.	03-02-45	Onie, Milton T.
13-06-43	McPherson, Dean C.	10-10-43	Paczolt, Steve
07-05-45	McPherson, Gana E.	27-05-43	Palmer, Louis
17-08-43	Mears, Kenneth J.	12-07-44	Paolantonic, George J.
12-07-44	Meinke, Robert	28-07-43	Parker, William J.
28-01-45	Mercer, Robert V.	14-05-43	Pascoe, Arthur R.
11-04-44	Messmer, Warren K.	11-04-44	Passero, Angelo
27-05-43	Metzger, Frank A.	28-07-43	Paul, Alonzo G.
16-08-44	Michael, Donald K.	14-05-43	Payne, John A.
11-12-43	Miller, Douglas J.	06-09-43	Peacock, Charles B.
21-05-43	Miller, George E.	28-07-43	Peacock, James W.
11-06-43	Miller, Richard C.	06-02-44	Peay, Horace M.
13-06-43	Miller, Walter C.	24-02-44	Peckacek, George F.
21-02-44	Miner, Arden L.	16-12-44	Pellow, Robert W.
19-07-44	Mintz, Victor L.	11-12-43	Pernira, Augusto
19-11-43	Mirabel, Louise M.	03-03-45	Peter, Edwin D.
18-02-43	Missana, Charles	03-02-45	Peterson, Kenneth L.
18-02-43	Mitska, Michael	28-09-44	Petrocene, Eugene
26-07-43	Mock, Donald E.	11-12-43	Petzack, Wallace
10-04-44	Moedebeck, Robert W.	11-04-44	Phillips, Edward L.
28-07-43	Moody, Eleazar L.	19-11-43	Phinney, Charles E.
29-12-43	Moon, Robert N.	13-06-43	Piatkowski, Chester L.
11-12-43	Moore, J.D.	09-10-43	Piispaneu, William E.
18-06-44	Moore, William J.	10-10-43	Piner, Ralph E.
17-08-43	Moorer, Earl J.	07-01-45	Pistak, Joseph
06-04-45	Morgan, Lawrence H.	10-02-44	Podolsky, Murray
18-02-43	Morris, George J.	03-02-45	Popisil, Leonard A.
03-02-45	Morris, Richard P.	28-07-43	Porter, Richard E.
20-12-43	Mowels, William H.	15-09-43	Prees, David F.
24-01-44	Mowers, Charles H.	10-07-43	Price, Arthur F.
29-12-43	Mullavey, Andrew J.	16-08-44	Price, Louis J.
10-01-45	Mullins, Charles S.	15-09-43	Provost, Raymond
16-08-44	Mullins, Omer C.	09-10-43	Queen, Walter H.

09-10-43	Rabinowitz, Lewis	11-04-44	Schiappacasse, Eugene
11-04-44	Radcliffe, James J.	30-11-44	Schmolke, Robert E.
30-07-43	Randall, Robert	21-05-43	Schnebly, Dexter C.
11-04-44	Rashead, Phillip M.	10-10-43	Schneider, Jerome B.
03-02-45	Ratts, Dean M.	13-06-43	Schwagel, Frank A.
14-05-43	Readding, Russell B.	13-06-43	Scott, Austin B.
12-07-44	Redin, James S.	12-08-43	Scott, Churchill L.
12-07-44	Reed, John R.	11-06-44	Scully, Charles H.
18-06-44	Reed, Phillip M.	10-02-44	Semerski, Michael
06-02-44	Rees, Harry	10-01-45	Setterfield, William
13-06-43	Reever, Floyd C.	28-09-44	Sevald, Tom
28-07-43	Regan, Francis J.	29-12-43	Shade, Harry A.
16-12-44	Reid, Thomas J.	28-07-43	Shafer, Robert T.
29-12-43	Remo, Louis G.	14-06-44	Shafer, William M.
13-06-43	Renaud, William G.	13-06-43	Sharpe, Bernard D.
07-05-45	Repiscak, Joseph P.	24-05-44	Sheehan, William T.
15-09-43	Rice, Rex A.	22-12-43	Short, Jack B.
13-06-43	Richardson, John A.	25-07-43	Sieg, Robert L.
19-11-43	Richmond, Gail A.	24-01-43	Simpson, Carl
23-03-45	Richter, William C.	14-05-43	Skwist, Frank A.
10-02-44	Ridley, Gus	25-07-43	Skylar, Henry
04-03-44	Rife, Henry	10-02-44	Sliwka, John
13-06-43	Rife, Wayne E.	10-10-43	Sluder, Richard W.
10-10-43	Rightmire, Roy E.	11-04-44	Smecik, Thomas A.
13-06-43	Riley, Harley H.	24-04-44	Smiley, Charles S.
17-08-43	Riley, John H.	26-07-43	Smith, Graham H.
11-12-43	Ritter, Marvin B.	14-05-43	Smith, James M.
30-11-44	Rives, Alfred	12-08-44	Smith, Loris R.
24-04-44	Roderick, Joseph E.	12-07-44	Smith, Richard S.
27-05-43	Rogers, Earl C.	02-08-44	Sohm, Frank T.
19-11-43	Rongstad, Kenneth B.	19-11-43	Soreason, Gordon V.
24-05-44	Rosenberg, Norman S.	11-12-43	Spangenberg, Milton C.
15-09-43	Roth, Frank A.	11-12-43	Sparks, Harold E.
12-07-44	Rozek, Robert R.	14-06-44	Spears, Walter A.
13-06-43	Rubin, Charles	13-06-43	Spellman, Graydon V.
10-07-43	Rudnick, Leonard A.	31-12-44	Spencer, Hyrum L.
11-04-44	Rudnicky, John J.	19-11-43	Spicer, Joseph F.
11-12-43	Rybolt, Donald L.	29-12-43	Spitzer, Kingsley F.
31-12-44	Saakfeld, Richard C.	11-12-43	Stanbery, Edward R.
24-02-44	Sahner, Clifford D.	29-01-45	Standt, Charles T.
26-07-43	Sandberg, Richard R.	28-07-43	Starkebaum, George B.
10-07-43	Sarchet, James R.	06-02-44	Starns, William D.
19-07-44	Sasser, James D.	29-01-44	Staudt, Charles T.
11-04-44	Saunders, Frank J.	18-06-44	Stevens, Darrell L.
13-06-43	Scavotto, Donald V.	18-02-43	Stevens, Howard D.
07-05-45	Sceurman, Lionel N.	06-04-45	Stice, Archie L.

13-06-43	Stirwalt, Harry A.	27-05-43	Welch, Howard R.
13-06-43	Stone, Austin V.	14-06-44	Wells, Goodwin S.
19-11-43	Straw, Warren M.	04-03-44	Wesp, John P.
26-07-43	Suess, Herbert F.	25-08-44	Whilhelm, Melvin F.
07-01-45	Sul, Edward I.	18-02-43	White, James D.
27-05-43	Swartz, Glenn W.	14-05-43	White, James L.
28-01-45	Taylor, Charles R.	30-11-44	Wicker, Charles C.
04-10-43	Taylor, Edgar S.	13-06-43	Wilder, Alan W.
11-04-44	Taylor, Gerald	28-07-43	Wilderson, Samuel L.
24-05-44	Temple, Robert I.	13-06-43	Wilkinson, Richard L.
11-04-44	Terry, Phillip D.	15-09-43	Willis, Robert H.
13-06-43	Thimm, Walter J.	11-04-44	Willveil, Samuel L.
07-10-44	Thomas, Dean P.	10-02-44	Wilson, Henry H.
29-12-43	Thomas, Linus C.	11-04-44	Wilson, Irving
16-08-44	Thomas, Lorie C.	13-06-43	Wilson, Wendell K.
10-04-44	Thompson, Ronald B.	09-10-43	Wing, Robert D.
16-08-43	Tillson, Ned W.	04-03-44	Winter, John H.
13-06-43	Timko, John J.	03-03-45	Wirth, Harvey A.
19-11-43	Torck, Julis	07-01-45	Wisner, Jess P.
14-05-43	Trent, Cecil G.	13-06-43	Wisznoski, Jack J.
13-06-43	Triches, Angelo	13-11-43	Witbeck, Charles O.
10-02-44	Trouse, Harold E.	29-12-43	Witt, Alden R.
27-05-43	Twiford, Jack S.	10-02-44	Wojciechowski, John J.
13-06-43	Vacek, August R.	05-11-44	Wolfson, James D.
11-06-43	Vail, John J.	11-06-43	Wood, Eugene W.
16-12-44	Vediner, Neil E.	04-03-44	Wood, Glenn E.
29-12-43	Verbuleez, Wendell	13-06-43	Wood, Hubert C.
20-12-43	Vollbrecht, Thomas R.	03-02-45	Wood, Kenneth C.
13-06-43	Wagner, Marvis L.	24-01-43	Woodward, E. E.
18-02-43	Walker, Oliver L.	11-04-44	Wright, Gardner W.
02-08-44	Walrod, Oscar C.	07-01-45	Wright, Richard L.
13-06-43	Walter, Cebert C.	12-08-44	Yablonski, Edwin M.
07-05-45	Walteri, George G.	13-06-43	York, Drakeford L.
12-07-44	Ward, James W.	24-01-43	Young, Haskill S.
10-02-44	Wardell, Arthur W.	14-06-44	Young, Orman W.
14-06-44	Warren, Burleigh W.	07-01-45	Yuille, William N.
26-07-43	Warshaver, Irwing B.	26-07-43	Zapatka, Frederick J.
03-02-45	Watt, William T.	13-06-43	Zwisner, Mylan F.
28-07-43	Weaver, Ernest E.		

All of the above names are men who gave their lives while flying in the 95th Bombardment Group. There were a total of 611 men killed in the line of duty. In addition, another 851 crew members were taken as prisoners of war. 171 men returned to the base as severely wounded. 65 men were interned in Sweden and Switzerland and another 61 were shot down and evaded capture behind enemy lines.

Epilogue

These losses were sustained only by the 95th B.G. There were a total of 30 groups of heavy bombers in England using the B-17 and the B-24. Add all of the fighter groups and the light and medium attack bombers and one can see the cost that the 8th Air Force paid. There were more casualties in the 8th A.F. than all other fighting units combined, including the U.S. Army and the U.S. Navy.